THE
WORLD
TRADE
CENTER

BUILDING
HISTORY
SERIES

THE WORLD TRADE CENTER

by Laurel Corona

LUCENT BOOKS
SAN DIEGO, CALIFORNIA

THOMSON

GALE

Detroit • New York • San Diego • San Francisco
Boston • New Haven, Conn. • Waterville, Maine
London • Munich

On cover: The top floors of the World Trade Center under construction (left); the Twin Towers at night (upper right); the lower
floors under construction (lower right).

Library of Congress Cataloging-in-Publication Data

Corona, Laurel, 1949–
    The World Trade Center / by Laurel Corona.
        p.   cm. — (Building history)
    Includes bibliographical references and index.
Summary: Discusses the history and construction of the massive
World Trade Center, daily operations, and the tragic events of
September 11, 2001.
        ISBN 1-59018-214-6
        1. World Trade Center (New York, N.Y.)—Juvenile literature.
2. Skyscrapers—New York (State)—New York—Juvenile litera-
ture. 3. New York (N.Y.)—Buildings, structures, etc.—Juvenile lit-
erature. [1. World Trade Center (New York, N.Y.) 2. Skyscrapers.
3. New York (N.Y.)—Buildings, structures, etc.] I. Title.   II. Series.
    NA6233.N5 C764 2002
    974.7' 1004—dc21

2001007834

CONTENTS

FOREWORD

Throughout history, as civilizations have evolved and prospered, each has produced unique buildings and architectural styles. Combining the need for both utility and artistic expression, a society's buildings, particularly its large-scale public structures, often reflect the individual character traits that distinguish it from other societies. In a very real sense, then, buildings express a society's values and unique characteristics in tangible form. As scholar Anita Abramovitz comments in her book *People and Spaces*, "Our ways of living and thinking—our habits, needs, fear of enemies, aspirations, materialistic concerns, and religious beliefs—have influenced the kinds of spaces that we build and that later surround and include us."

That specific types and styles of structures constitute an outward expression of the spirit of an individual people or era can be seen in the diverse ways that various societies have built palaces, fortresses, tombs, churches, government buildings, sports arenas, public works, and other such monuments. The ancient Greeks, for instance, were a supremely rational people who originated Western philosophy and science, including the atomic theory and the realization that the earth is a sphere. Their public buildings, epitomized by Athens's magnificent Parthenon temple, were equally rational, emphasizing order, harmony, reason, and above all, restraint.

By contrast, the Romans, who conquered and absorbed the Greek lands, were a highly practical people preoccupied with acquiring and wielding power over others. The Romans greatly admired and readily copied elements of Greek architecture, but modified and adapted them to their own needs. "Roman genius was called into action by the enormous practical needs of a world empire," wrote historian Edith Hamilton. "Rome met them magnificently. Buildings tremendous, indomitable, amphitheaters where eighty thousand could watch a spectacle, baths where three thousand could bathe at the same time."

In medieval Europe, God heavily influenced and motivated the people, and religion permeated all aspects of society, molding people's worldviews and guiding their everyday actions. That spiritual mindset is reflected in the most important medieval structure—the Gothic cathedral—which, in a sense, was a model of heavenly cities. As scholar Anne Fremantle so elegantly phrases it, the cathedrals were "harmonious elevations of stone and glass reaching up to heaven to seek and receive the light [of God]."

Our more secular modern age, in contrast, is driven by the realities of a global economy, advanced technology, and mass communications. Responding to the needs of international trade and the growth of cities housing millions of people, today's builders construct engineering marvels, among them towering skyscrapers of steel and glass, mammoth marine canals, and huge and elaborate rapid transit systems, all of which would have left their ancestors, even the Romans, awestruck.

In examining some of humanity's greatest edifices, Lucent Books' Building History series recognizes this close relationship between a society's historical character and its buildings. Each volume in the series begins with a historical sketch of the people who erected the edifice, exploring their major achievements as well as the beliefs, customs, and societal needs that dictated the variety, functions, and styles of their buildings. A detailed explanation of how the selected structure was conceived, designed, and built, to the extent that this information is known, makes up the majority of the volume.

Each volume in the Lucent Building History series also includes several special features that are useful tools for additional research. A chronology of important dates gives students an overview, at a glance, of the evolution and use of the structure described. Sidebars create a broader context by adding further details on some of the architects, engineers, and construction tools, materials, and methods that made each structure a reality, as well as the social, political, and/or religious leaders and movements that inspired its creation. Useful maps help the reader locate the nations, cities, streets, and individual structures mentioned in the text; and numerous diagrams and pictures illustrate tools and devices that bring to life various stages of construction. Finally, each volume contains two bibliographies, one for student research, the other listing works the author consulted in compiling the book.

Taken as a whole, these volumes, covering diverse ancient and modern structures, constitute not only a valuable research tool, but also a tribute to the human spirit, a fascinating exploration of the dreams, skills, ingenuity, and dogged determination of the great peoples who shaped history.

Important Dates in the Building of the World Trade Center

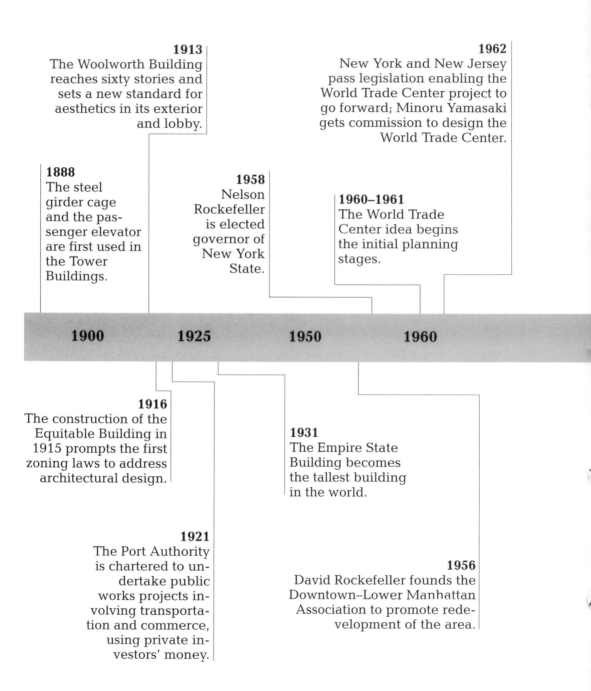

1913
The Woolworth Building reaches sixty stories and sets a new standard for aesthetics in its exterior and lobby.

1962
New York and New Jersey pass legislation enabling the World Trade Center project to go forward; Minoru Yamasaki gets commission to design the World Trade Center.

1888
The steel girder cage and the passenger elevator are first used in the Tower Buildings.

1958
Nelson Rockefeller is elected governor of New York State.

1960–1961
The World Trade Center idea begins the initial planning stages.

1900   1925   1950   1960

1916
The construction of the Equitable Building in 1915 prompts the first zoning laws to address architectural design.

1931
The Empire State Building becomes the tallest building in the world.

1921
The Port Authority is chartered to undertake public works projects involving transportation and commerce, using private investors' money.

1956
David Rockefeller founds the Downtown–Lower Manhattan Association to promote redevelopment of the area.

1968
The laying of the first grillage signals the official beginning of the erection of the towers.

1970
The north tower, Tower 1, "tops out"; the first tenants move in to the uncompleted building.

1993
A bomb explodes in the World Trade Center's basement parking structure, killing six people.

1967
Construction of the "bathtub" begins, using the slurry trench method.

2001
The World Trade Center is destroyed in a terrorist attack.

1965   1970   1980   1990   2000

1971
The south tower tops out.

1998
The operation of the World Trade Center is turned over by Port Authority to a private leaseholder.

1966
The last challenges to the World Trade Center are effectively countered by Port Authority; wrecking crews begin demolition; excavation begins on the World Trade Center site; Battery Park City begins receiving landfill.

1973
The World Trade Center is officially dedicated.

Introduction

This is not computer animation," CBS News anchor Dan Rather kept repeating. "This is real footage."[1] To a nation in which movie studios routinely churn out remarkably realistic scenes of destruction, a plane heading into a skyscraper, which explodes into flames, and then falls in a cloud of dust that billows out over city streets crowded with fleeing people, may have seemed like something from a movie whose name one could not quite remember. What it could not be was real footage from a bystander's video camera. But it was. On the morning of September 11, 2001, reality outstripped even the most vivid imagination. Two buildings and approximately three thousand people shared the same fate and now lay together in a seven-story-high pile of debris. A stunned nation was in the grips of one of the most important events, and defining moments, in its history.

An American Icon

Before the events of September 11, 2001, the World Trade Center was already part of that history, already an icon. The center was designed to include the two tallest buildings in the world, known informally as the Twin Towers and officially as Towers 1 and 2. It also was meant to serve as a visual reminder to everyone at home and abroad of American technological superiority, economic strength, and faith in America's future. For almost three decades, the towers dominated the skyline of Manhattan, the "City of Skyscrapers." The heap of smoldering rubble left behind in the aftermath of the terrorist attack, and the phantom outlines of the Twin Towers that remain in the imaginations of those who look at the New York skyline today, remain icons, although of a different kind. What were once two proud exclamation points rising between the Hudson and East Rivers have given way to a question mark as America struggles to make sense of what happened, and what it means for the future.

Taller than the surrounding skyscrapers and isolated from other structures by the large plaza at their base, the Twin Towers perhaps stood for something else in addition to America's economic and political strength. Of all the buildings in New York, the towers were in some respects the easiest to hit precisely because of their height and their isolation. People around the world who resent and even passionately hate the United

States do so largely because of these two qualities. America is rich and powerful but also, some argue, out of touch with the rest of the world and unaware of how its high standard of living has been achieved in part by exploiting the people and resources of poorer countries. The terrorists who cut the planes, and the lives aboard them, into ribbons at the Twin Towers were, in a symbolic sense, trying to cut America down to size.

MOVING FORWARD

While bulldozers still remove the debris, loved ones mourn the dead, and nearby shop owners and residents tend to shattered windows as well as shattered confidence, talk has begun about what should take the World Trade Center's place. But as philosopher George Santayana once said, those who forget the past are condemned to repeat it. If Santayana's warning is to be heeded, how the idea of the World Trade Center evolved—the almost incomprehensible complexity of building a skyscraper at all, much less so massive a structure in a densely built and heavily trafficked

Before their destruction, the Twin Towers of the World Trade Center dwarfed the other buildings in the Manhattan skyline.

neighborhood—and how the project affected the area in which it stood is an important story to tell. The World Trade Center was controversial, and some say illegal, when it was planned and built. Its exterior appearance received little praise at the time, although it did win general acceptance as the years passed. And its architecture undoubtedly contributed to its collapse. In addition, many say that America has moved on from the need to build bigger and higher. They argue in favor of projects that do not challenge the outer edges of human capability but instead offer a warmer invitation to come and linger, projects that reflect a better understanding of human scale.

AMERICAN PRIDE

The resilience of the American people and the extent of their pride in their way of life, as shown in the aftermath of the disaster, may have come as a surprise to some around the world, but not to Americans themselves. Americans have a clear sense that who they are is men and women of all colors, religions, and lands of origin who, by their hands and their heads, shaped and continue to shape a country. They do not tend to define themselves by their buildings or even by the history that those buildings represent but, rather, by their quality of life in the here and now and by the concepts that guide them, including the treasured belief that freedom means they can create their own destinies. This way of thinking was at the heart of the activities in the 1950s and '60s that brought the World Trade Center into existence. The World Trade Center was intended to improve the quality of life in Manhattan, and it was supposed to symbolize progress. It was built by people, from bank presidents to crane operators, with a profound sense that, to have what they wanted, they had to dream big and work hard.

On that site in Lower Manhattan, the ingenuity, risk taking, problem solving, and physical skills of thousands of people came together, and the best and worst about human nature were displayed. In the aftermath of September 11, it seems likely that the rise from the ashes will be the same story told again.

The Shaping
of a City

When the Dutch West India Company first began exploring the American continent in 1624, it came across a massive natural harbor into which two strong rivers flowed. Between these two rivers was an island of forests and meadows, home to small villages of Algonquian Indians. Carpeted with snow in the winter and wildflowers in the spring, it was also filled with abundant wildlife that sustained the Algonquin people.

But the Dutch were looking for something more than a place to live. Their vision was focused in two opposite directions: back across the Atlantic to Europe and its markets and forward into the interior of the American continent, where products for those markets could be found. For the Dutch, the island now known as Manhattan, one of the five boroughs of New York City, was a perfect place for those two visions to become one. The rivers would enable them to use boats, by far the easiest form of travel, to reach deep into the interior and come back laden with furs and other products to put on ships bound back across the ocean to Holland and other European countries.

In a story well known to many American schoolchildren, in 1626 Peter Minuit, the director of the New Netherlands colony established by the Dutch West India Company, bargained with the Indians for the right to create a permanent colony on fourteen thousand acres of land between what later became known as the Hudson and East Rivers. The Indians, who had no concept of ownership of land, accepted beads and trinkets in exchange for their agreement to let the Dutch stay. The concept of land as real estate, a thing whose value can be measured in money, an asset that can be bought and sold, entered into American history at that moment.

13

The director of New Netherlands, Peter Minuit, offers Indians beads and trinkets in exchange for the fourteen thousand acres which would later become Manhattan.

Nearly four centuries later, trinkets are still sold in Manhattan. Many of them depict the Twin Towers of the World Trade Center, two of the most recognized buildings in the world during their three decades of existence. Though they and other skyscrapers such as the Empire State Building served as symbols of American progress and success, the essential truth remains: They were, in the end, real estate ventures for profit, just as the meadows of seventeenth-century Manhattan were for the Dutch. The Dutch went up the Hudson River in search of riches. Their counterparts in the twentieth century went up into the sky.

RAILROADS, FACTORIES, AND IMMIGRANTS

The dual vision of the Dutch settlers continued to be a factor in the development of New York. By the nineteenth century, New York had long been the most important port in the United States, not just because of its excellent natural harbor but because its easternmost location cut the distance, and thus the length of the journey, across the Atlantic Ocean by one day. Products destined for Europe, therefore, almost inevitably passed through New York harbor on their journey. Increasingly, people seeking a better life in the United States also passed through the harbor to the immigration terminal at Ellis Island. In 1886, New York's role as the center for immigration was acknowledged by the dedication of the Statue of Liberty in its harbor, with its inscription beckoning the tired and poor of the world to seek new lives of freedom in America.

At the same time that immigration was increasing, so was technology. The nineteenth century saw the birth of the factory. The ability to mass-produce items such as clothing and other household goods led to the development of sweatshops, which employed thousands of people whose lack of special skills or command of the English language made other employment options limited. As a result, more and more immigrants came to New York because jobs were plentiful. Many lived in Lower Manhattan, in the area around what is today Chinatown and Little Italy.

Immigrants and factories were not the only forces converging on New York in the nineteenth century. A third element that shaped the New York of today was the railroad. With the railroad, large quantities of materials could be shipped across the continent. This affected New York in particular, because more products that were ultimately destined for overseas markets could reach their last North American stopping point on the docks of New York harbor more quickly. There they would be loaded onto the newer and bigger vessels of the first transoceanic shipping lines. Enterprising people such as John Pierpont Morgan built fortunes by privately funding railroad and shipping lines, projects that they saw as benefiting not only themselves but the country as a whole.

JOHN PIERPONT MORGAN

No name is more synonymous with the growth of New York as a financial center and a major hub of world trade than John Pierpont Morgan. In an era when the penny still had purchasing power, Morgan was one of the world's first billionaires.

John Pierpont Morgan was one of America's first billionaires.

John Pierpont Morgan was born in Hartford, Connecticut, in 1837 into a wealthy banking family. By age thirty-five, he was already in charge of a complex network of banking and business interests with combined assets and spending power greater than that of the entire U.S. government. In 1901, he bought the Carnegie Steel Company for $480 million when the federal budget totaled only $300 million. This purchase allowed him to merge his own Federal Steel Company with Carnegie Steel, creating the world's first billion-dollar company, United States Steel. Morgan's fortune and business sense were so important to the American economy that funds from his banking interests were used to bail out the U.S. government and the stock market during financial crises.

Morgan's astronomical wealth was certainly enhanced by the skyscraper boom, because the buildings required massive amounts of steel, which his company could provide. He also invested heavily in railroads, great users of steel for both the tracks and the trains. The railroads were also the means by which American commerce could grow, and a way New York could develop into the most financially and commercially important city in the world.

Though Morgan always looked out for his own interests, he was keenly aware that a healthy American economy was essential for him to keep making money. He also felt strongly about philanthropy; he funded the construction of the Cathedral of St. John the Divine and founded various museums. Throughout his life, he collected art and books, and upon his death, his personal collection was used to fill the Morgan Library and one wing of the Metropolitan Museum of Art. He died in 1913.

Manhattan was bursting with energy, money, and people as the nineteenth century drew to a close. Its two greatest assets to the Dutch, the river and the harbor, had become mixed blessings because, unlike in many other American cities, there was no place to expand. People crowded into tenements, walking up many floors to dingy and crowded apartments without running water. Businesses wanting to be in the thick of commercial activity had difficulty finding office space in Lower Manhattan, because no building rose higher than the few floors people would be willing to walk up, and there was no more land on which to erect new buildings. As the twentieth century neared, New York seemed to be choking on its own success. If it were going to find relief, it would have to find a way to build higher.

IDIOCY OR INSPIRATION?

The problem in building higher lay largely in the materials available for constructing buildings. At that time, walls were generally made of brick, or what builders call masonry. Masonry walls are sturdy, but they must be built thick enough to support the weight of the stories above them. It was clear that building higher with brick was going to result in walls on the lower floors being so thick that the amount of open space for offices would be reduced to an unprofitable level. A new material would have to be used. Inspiration came from France, where the highly original and controversial Eiffel Tower was under construction for the Universal Exposition of 1889. There, visitors were whisked up on the newly invented elevator to a viewing platform high above the city. The structure itself was nothing more than a metal frame, its beams and supports forming a graceful sculptural tribute to the power of steel to scrape the sky.

John Stearns, "a young silk merchant with real estate dreams"[2] was one of those impressed by reports of Gustave Eiffel's accomplishment. He had plans to turn a vacant lot in midtown Manhattan into a profitable office building. He turned to architect Bradford L. Gilbert to help him accomplish his goal. Gilbert decided to try an untested method of construction, a network of steel columns and crossbars known as a girder cage, to reinforce the walls of the planned thirteen-story building. The Tower Building, as it was named, was by far the tallest building in New York when it was completed in 1888, and it had an even better than average amount of rentable office space despite its extra height. According to author Eric Darton,

> In the face of public belief that his experiment would topple over in a stiff breeze, Gilbert moved his own offices into the top floor of the proto-skyscraper that popular skepticism had renamed the Idiotic Building. Soon afterward, a full-scale hurricane descended on the city. In its aftermath, reporters rushed to write up the ruins. But not a brick of the Idiotic Building had fallen.[3]

The steel girder cage would become the new industry standard. The cage and the elevators needed to bring people to the upper floors were the two new developments that unleashed a frenzy of building taller and taller structures in Manhattan.

These earliest tall buildings did not last long even though they were solidly built. They fell to wrecking balls as technology, experience, and confidence grew. Soon, what had seemed a few decades before like a remarkable amount of office space in these buildings was not nearly enough to make a profit, because the overall value of land in Manhattan had soared along with the height of the buildings.

Within only a quarter of a century, in 1913, the Woolworth Building rose to the as-yet-unprecedented height of sixty stories. By then, even though the steel girder cage was more than adequate to support that

Although skeptics had nicknamed the Tower Building (pictured) the Idiotic Building, architect Bradford L. Gilbert's innovative design proved them wrong.

height, new technologies were needed to enable going up that high, and to support the services required in the building once it was completed. New scaffolding techniques and hoists had to be developed to put the building together. According to author Eric Darton, "sewage pipes wide enough to accommodate a horse and carriage and a generator churning out electrical power for [the equivalent of] a city of fifty thousand"[4] also had to be part of the building plans. Sinking massive amounts of their personal fortunes into the construction of such buildings was soon perceived as a good business investment by those who could afford it. Little by little, the focus of the richest men in America was shifting from railroads to real estate.

THE 1916 ZONING CODE

Covered with granite and terra cotta and stunningly decorated inside, the appearance of the Woolworth Building prompted preacher Samuel Parkes Cadman to call it the "Cathedral of Commerce,"[5] for he felt its beauty and size made it the equivalent to business what the cathedrals of Europe were to religion. The Equitable Building was another such "cathedral" built around the same time. Though not as tall, it was more massive, rising straight up from the street to its full forty-story height. The Equitable Building produced thirty-nine times its land area in rentable office space, more than twice that of the more aesthetically designed Woolworth Building.

However, whereas people generally liked the Woolworth Building, few had anything positive to say about the Equitable Building. Many saw it as a sign of bad things to come if rules were not enacted about what could and could not be built in Manhattan. The main problem with the Equitable Building was that its mass at the higher levels obscured the sky, and if other buildings followed suit, the streets of Manhattan would be perpetually dark. More important to businesses was the fact that natural light and table lamps were the only means by which buildings were lit. The overhead lighting of today had yet to be invented. For an office to be usable, it had to be close to a window, and there had to be light coming through those windows.

In 1916, New York City adopted its first comprehensive code for zoning of property. This code not only determined what could be built where but also established limitations on building design. The code was based on a mathematical formula involving the size of the building site and the relationship of height, mass, and rentable floor space of what was to be built on it. No longer could the entire air space above a building site be obliterated by the structure put on it. Future skyscrapers such as the Empire State Building and the Chrysler Building, both built in the 1930s, are evidence of the farsightedness of this code. Each of these buildings employs setbacks, the term used for building designs that become narrower as they rise taller.

Although these first building codes were altered over the years, the same general idea prevailed: The taller one built, the more one had to protect the daylight that made being on the streets and in other office buildings tolerable. By the time the World Trade Center was proposed, the code was more specific about open space in relation to height, and the twin

This view of midtown Manhattan shows the huge Empire State Building (left) and the Chrysler Building (tallest building at right). Both buildings used setbacks as required by the zoning code established in 1916.

110-story towers were balanced by the inclusion of a huge plaza. This gave an airiness to the overall project that offset the twin 4-million-square-foot buildings perched over that sun-drenched public square.

BALANCING PUBLIC AND PRIVATE WEALTH

That people who lived and worked in areas with skyscrapers should not be negatively impacted by them became a well established principle in the decades that followed. By the time the World Trade Center was built, few would argue that those wealthy enough to buy land in the heart of a city could treat that land as theirs to do with entirely as they wished. There should be some benefit to the public or the project would simply seem greedy. The balance between private property and public responsibility is never more delicately played out than in projects the magnitude of the World Trade Center. This sense of public responsibility as a counterbalance to private profit was cultivated by the first zoning codes in New York, but it has its roots much deeper in the public parks and squares of old European cities, as well as the small towns of colonial America.

Perhaps the clearest illustration of the logic of linking the wealth of a few to the quality of life of the many is the Woolworth Building. Woolworth's was once a fixture in the small towns of America, where it was often known simply as the "five and dime" or the dime store. When the Woolworth Building was erected in Manhattan, it was clear that the nickels and dimes of average Americans had built a huge family fortune, one that, by virtue of the implication that it required such a building, would continue to grow. It made sense, therefore, that the building should be pleasing to the eye and thoughtfully planned, logic that the World Trade Center later embraced not just as a matter of code but of conscience and aesthetics. From the outside, the Woolworth Building looks like a whimsical castle tower complete with gargoyles and turrets. Inside, its public lobby features glass mosaics, gleaming polished steel doors with gold backgrounds, and lustrous marble walls. It is a destination in itself, available for all to enjoy.

ANOTHER KIND OF SHADOW

However, especially in cities, where luxury and hardship exist side by side, there are bound to be many who resent the wide gap between rich and poor. The carved figure of founder Frank

Woolworth counting his coins that decorates one corner of the Woolworth Building lobby may have amused and even inspired some who saw it. But many of those whose coins had helped finance the building lived in crowded walk-ups with peeling, water-stained walls; the lavishly decorated building merely served as a

THE COMPETITION: THE EMPIRE STATE BUILDING

According to Eric P. Nash, author of *Manhattan Skyscrapers*, the Empire State Building is "the one to which all others must inevitably be compared." For four decades, from 1931 until the completion of the World Trade Center towers, it was the tallest building in the world, crowning the New York City skyline like the spires of a cathedral in European cities. After the completion of the Twin Towers, the Empire State Building promoted itself not as the tallest but as the most famous skyscraper in the world. In fact, it continued to draw more visitors than the Twin Towers, largely because of its association with movies such as the original *King Kong*, *An Affair to Remember*, and *Sleepless in Seattle*. It is now once again the tallest building in New York.

One of the remarkable things about the Empire State Building is the speed at which it was built. Averaging a little less than five floors a week, the building was completely finished in a year and a half. It is built of bricks—10 million of them—and 200,000 cubic feet of stone in setbacks, in which the first stories serve as a platform for the first section of the high-rise. Above that, the next section is somewhat smaller, and so on. Atop the setbacks, the upper floors shoot straight up to approximately the eightieth floor, where the structure once again becomes smaller and is ultimately crowned with a huge, floodlit spire. This spire makes the building one of the most recognizable in the world, with or without King Kong hanging from it.

On July 28, 1945, a B-25 bomber drifted off course and struck the Empire State Building at around the seventy-ninth floor, setting off a massive fire and killing fourteen people. This event stayed in the minds of other high-rise architects. Indeed, the Twin Towers were later designed to withstand the impact of the typical passenger plane of the 1970s, which was smaller and carried less fuel than airplanes of the present era.

The Woolworth Building (center) and other skyscrapers became symbols of the disparity between rich and poor.

reminder of the way the Woolworths and others like them lived. To some, Manhattan represented what was wrong with the American dream more than what was right: Too many people lived poorly so that some could live very well. Thus, with the growth of skyscrapers also came a growth in political activism that often made these same skyscrapers—and the people who built them—its targets. Even though zoning codes could prevent one kind of shadow from engulfing Manhattan's streets, the economic disparities between rich and poor cast a shadow of another kind.

A LEGACY OF VIOLENCE

When William Norcross stood in the doorway of the offices of tycoon Russell Sage in 1888 and shouted "here goes!" before hurling a dynamite bomb into the lobby, he initiated a legacy of violence against symbols of wealth and power in New York. On July 4, 1914, while a fireworks display lit up the sky over New York harbor, four members of the International Workers of the World, a communist organization, accidentally blew themselves up a few miles away in Harlem with a bomb they had intended to use to kill John D. Rockefeller, one of the wealthiest men in the United States. Then, on September 16, 1920, a huge bomb hidden in a horse-drawn buggy exploded in front of the Wall Street bank owned by John Pierpont Morgan, the richest man in America.

Decades later, on February 26, 1993, an explosion twenty-two feet wide and five stories deep ripped through the parking area of the World Trade Center, killing six, injuring one thousand, and leaving fifty thousand stranded in the dark when the electricity went out. The bomb, hidden in a van, was intended to destroy the towers' foundations and bring down the buildings. Though it caused massive damage to the basement and lower floors, the damage was fully repaired in less than two months. Life at the World Trade Center went on much as before, except with a few more restrictions such as requiring passes for employees and temporary permits for all visitors to offices in the building, and ending parking in the basement for everyone except employees.

At the time, the bomb at the World Trade Center was the most destructive terrorist act ever committed on American soil. Bruce Hoffman, a terrorism specialist, said in an interview quoted by Angus Kress Gillespie in *Twin Towers: The Life of New York City's World Trade Center*, "A car bomb in a street in New York doubtless would have killed more people. But the World Trade Center is a symbol of Wall Street [the financial center of the United States] and the Manhattan skyline and the United States itself, and I think that is very important." So did the planners and implementers of the September 11, 2001, attack, which succeeded where the first plot had failed to bring the buildings to the ground.

Only a few months after the opening of the Tower Building in 1888, William Norcross, a man deemed a lunatic by many, threw a bomb into a neighboring building housing the offices of railroad and real estate tycoon Russell Sage. One person was killed and eight others injured. It was only the first of a number of bombings that have targeted Manhattan buildings and people who are symbols of wealth and power. Since then, the focus of the resentment has shifted from poor Americans against rich Americans to poorer people of the world against the United States as a whole. Nevertheless, the targets have remained the same.

The meadows and streams of Algonquin Manhattan have long since given way to beautiful public plazas as well as dilapidated and graffiti-ridden parks, white fountains with famous sculptures as well as open fire hydrants in ghettos on a hot summer day. Today, the skyscraper, once a symbol of progress and American superiority and a great source of national pride, is a symbol of a far more complex history and destiny. Its glass windows still reflect the world around it, but it is a far different world than was previously understood.

THE DEAL IS SEALED: PORT POLITICS

In the past, money could be made in New York because of its geographical location. As the twentieth century progressed, that situation changed. It is not that New York's location became unfavorable to trade; it remains one of the best-situated natural ports in the world. Rather, New York had become so important as a center of trade that its greatest asset was simply the fact that it was New York. It was the center of everything connected to making money, and people seeking to get ahead in business would pay top dollar just to live and do business there.

As New York became a magnet for business enterprises of all sorts, the way to make fortunes shifted to real estate. Increasingly, the powerful elite of the city, who had become rich by building the railroads and shipping lines that made New York the hub of commerce, began shifting their holdings away from railroads and industry. A new generation of Peter Minuits, now holding checkbooks instead of beads, wanted to buy Manhattan all over again and rebuild it to suit them. This would have a profound effect on the city, distancing it so effectively from the things that had built it in the first place. The wharves and ships soon became associated primarily with tourist and cultural attractions such as the South Street Seaport, invoking a lost past rather than the present.

SHAPING THE FUTURE OF MANHATTAN

By the 1960s, behind the closed doors of the most powerful figures in New York City, a complex struggle for wealth and power was being waged over the future of Lower Manhattan. Players in this game included the Port Authority, the governors of New

York and New Jersey, the mayor of New York City, and a dozen or more of the richest people in New York. At stake were several crucial issues, including the future of the port of New York and the use of land in Manhattan.

The idea of building a centralized complex in Manhattan to house businesses connected to worldwide trade was first raised in the 1940s. However, it seemed impossible to accomplish because there was nowhere to put it, and studies showed that the money could be better spent refurbishing and expanding the port. By the 1960s, however, a number of new developments had occurred and a world trade center was again the subject of active discussions over coffee in boardrooms and martinis in bars.

The first important development was the call for "urban renewal." This term refers to efforts, usually large-scale ones, to

A 1973 aerial photo shows the location of the World Trade Center in Lower Manhattan. The idea of building a complex housing businesses dealing in world trade had been conceived thirty years earlier.

make the centers of cities more attractive, more smoothly functioning, and more profitable. Lower Manhattan in the 1960s was perceived by many as an eyesore. Though it had its share of lovely neighborhoods and historic buildings, much of the land was filled with slums and low-rise buildings housing small, family-owned businesses. Urban planners promoted visions of how to rebuild Lower Manhattan literally from the ground up as a city of the future, replacing its congested, dirty, and often run-down streets with fast-moving expressways leading to massive shopping and business complexes. These would be rimmed by new and much improved housing, most of it not affordable to the poor, thus deliberately forcing them out to the suburbs in favor of more affluent residents.

Although probably no one genuinely believed that such an extreme scenario would ever come to pass, these visions did reinforce the idea that much of Lower Manhattan would have to

Slums like the one pictured here kept property values low in Lower Manhattan. Real estate investors wanted to get rid of slums to increase the potential for making money in the area.

be rebuilt if its real estate value were to be maximized. The two eyesores that seemed most likely to keep Lower Manhattan property values down were the shipping docks and the slums. To those interested in increasing the value of their current holdings and speculating further in Lower Manhattan real estate, both had to go.

THE PORT AUTHORITY

The second development feeding into the reborn idea of a world trade center was the changing emphasis of the Port Authority. Chartered in 1921, the Port Authority's job was to develop, coordinate, and oversee all transportation-related activities in the fifteen-hundred-square-mile area of New York and New Jersey falling within a twenty-five-mile radius of the Statue of Liberty. Subways, railroads, bridges, ferries, airports, and shipping terminals were all under Port Authority control. However, the Port Authority's interest had gradually shifted away from things such as building bridges, tunnels, and terminals. Its board had always consisted of some of the most successful businesspeople in New York, and they were looking for ways to serve both the public interest and their own desire for profit.

In the eyes of many, the Port Authority did not handle its obligation to the people of New York very well during the 1960s. For example, the port of New York was handicapped by the fact that there was no rail tunnel under the Hudson River. Trains had to stop in New Jersey and move their transatlantic cargo across the Hudson by other means. As a result, shipping terminals had sprung up in New Jersey and elsewhere, diverting business from New York and thus costing jobs and harming the economy. Though building a rail tunnel was proclaimed as a main priority for the Port Authority, none was ever built. In part, this was because the elite of New York really did not want the port revitalized. Train and shipping terminals tend to be ugly and they take up a lot of space, space that could be used more profitably as commercial real estate. But the main reason the tunnel was not built was that, by then, many leading figures in government and finance had decided they wanted to use the power of the Port Authority to build a world trade center instead.

The Port Authority was supposed to act in the public interest to build projects benefiting the public directly. It financed projects by issuing bonds that were eventually repaid by those who used the projects—for example, by paying bridge tolls and sub-way fares. Private investors put their own money into the con-struction, which promised a good return for their investment upon the completion of the project. Taxpayers did not directly fund these projects, but most did not realize that investors were guaranteed repayment from tax revenues if the project failed to return their investment.

Because the Port Authority was not an office of the govern-ment and its members were not elected by the public, it could operate as it wished, funding or not funding projects at will, pro-vided that it followed its charter. Problems began to arise when Port Authority officials began looking at a clause in the charter that gave them "full power and authority to purchase, construct, lease, and operate terminal, transportation and other facilities of commerce within the port district."[6] Though the Port Authority was not supposed to speculate in real estate, perhaps, its board reasoned, if a project were specifically designed to pull together "facilities of commerce," it would not be against the charter to build a great complex in which trade-related businesses could work side by side. Such a complex would also replace many city blocks of unattractive and unprofitable buildings and could serve as the centerpiece for the revitalization of Lower Manhat-tan. Thus, the idea for the World Trade Center was born.

SELLING THE IDEA

The project would prove a hard sell to just about everyone. The size, nature, and location of the World Trade Center changed over the years in order to appease everyone with the power to undercut the proposal. Ultimately, this caused a climate of criti-cism that hovered over the project its entire life. For example, the mayor of New York City, Robert Wagner Jr., was opposed to the idea because all Port Authority projects operate tax free. The World Trade Center would impact the city but would not pay into its operating costs. In truth, he could not have stopped the Port Authority from approving the project, nor could he have stopped it from buying up the square blocks needed to build it. However, Wagner did hold a trump card: The city controlled the streets, and there would be no tearing up or rerouting of streets without city approval. To get the mayor's go-ahead, the Port Au-thority had to agree to reimburse the city for the projected losses in tax revenue.

The governor of New Jersey, Richard J. Hughes, had his own problems with the World Trade Center. The Port Authority was obligated to give equivalent treatment to New Jersey and New York in its projects. Hughes looked at the proposal, noted that the center was to be placed on the southeastern corner of Manhattan, and questioned what was in it for his state. He pointed out that the Port Authority had more pressing matters to deal with than launching this venture, including the financial rescue and revitalization of the Hudson and Manhattan Commuter Railroad that linked New Jersey and Lower Manhattan. However, he added, if this subway project were undertaken at the same time, New Jersey would go along with the World Trade Center idea.

New York City mayor Robert Wagner Jr. opposed the World Trade Center because, like all Port Authority projects, it would not be required to pay taxes to the city.

This prompted a momentous shift in the Port Authority's plans. It decided that the best way to accomplish both goals was to move the site of the World Trade Center across Manhattan to the Lower West Side, where the terminal of the subway line was located. The Port Authority would build a new terminal under the World Trade Center for the renamed Port Authority Trans-Hudson (PATH) trains, and the increased passenger volume generated by the tenants of the new center would guarantee its profitability.

The question for the Port Authority was not whether New York's mayor and the governor of New Jersey would support the project in the end; rather, it was how much (and exactly what) creating a "win-win" situation was going to cost. Private citizens, however, had their own worries and found that they had far less to bargain with. For example, Harry Helmsley, the owner of the Empire State Building, pointed out that a huge new office complex was not needed because existing midtown high rises were not even at full occupancy. Empty office space drives down lease prices, the opposite of what the commercial real estate speculators were trying to accomplish.

Though Helmsley's money made him powerful enough to be listened to and appeased, others were not so fortunate. For many, the saddest part of the saga of building the World Trade Center is the

"Mr. Small Businessman" rests in a coffin on Radio Row. Electronics shop owners protest the destruction of their businesses to make way for the World Trade Center.

story of Radio Row. No one would have argued that Radio Row was aesthetically appealing, but it represented something beautiful to the families who owned and operated the electronics shops that lined its streets and gave the neighborhood its nickname. Here, hard work had led to the modest success of financial independence and the promise of a better life for the next generation. When it was agreed that the location of the World Trade Center would be moved west, Radio Row was doomed. Even though some Radio Row businesses doggedly mounted legal challenges, one by one, properties were bought up and demolished. The promised financial and relocation help either did not materialize or was not enough, and many Radio Row families lost their homes and businesses.

A DESIGN EMERGES

Those who had supported the World Trade Center had done so without seeing any specific plans for the completed site. It was not that the plans were secret. They simply did not exist. When Minoru Yamasaki competed for and eventually was awarded the contract as project architect in 1962, he was given general parameters as to how much office, retail, parking, and other kinds of space were required, but beyond that, he was free to play around with different ideas, subject to Port Authority approval. Yamasaki created a scale model of Lower Manhattan in his Detroit office, complete with all existing buildings and an empty space where the World Trade Center site was located. Then he experimented with different shapes, sizes, and numbers of buildings.

Yamasaki's favorite design was two eighty-story towers in a plaza with several smaller buildings. The towers were situated in such a way that both could be seen regardless of where one stood,

THE FIGHT TO SAVE RADIO ROW

Before 1966, the merchants of Radio Row may have paid only a little attention to the news that a gigantic World Trade Center would be built on the east side of Lower Manhattan. In 1966, however, the situation changed dramatically when they learned that the location had been shifted to the West Side and that Radio Row was right in the middle of the new site. The electronics shop owners and other merchants vowed to fight. Led by Oscar Nadel, whose business, Oscar's Radio, had been open since 1920, they formed the Downtown West Businessmen's Association (DWBA) to combat the Port Authority and David Rockefeller's similarly named Downtown–Lower Manhattan Association.

Oscar Nadel truly believed that if the public and the courts were presented with the facts about the World Trade Center's true purpose as a commercial real estate project, the World Trade Center could be stopped in its tracks before Radio Row fell victim. Rallies featuring protesters carrying the coffin of "Mr. Small Businessman" got media attention and embarrassed David Rockefeller's brother Nelson's campaign for president in 1964. Meanwhile, legal challenges made their way all the way to the U.S. Supreme Court.

The legal argument was based on the point that the condemnation of their land and their forced removal from it was not for a public purpose. This principle, known as eminent domain, says that anyone's land can be taken—with reasonable compensation—by the government to build something such as a freeway or a state building. The DWBA told the courts that the project was simply a disguised real estate venture and that they therefore had the same rights anyone has to refuse to sell their property just because someone wants to buy it. The Port Authority scrambled to put together a counterargument that, in retrospect, clearly was not entirely truthful. Port Authority officials swore that their only motive was the proper one of building a center to promote commerce in New York, adding that it could also serve as a government building for any offices wishing to locate there.

The merchants of Radio Row lost appeal after appeal all the way to the Supreme Court. The wrecking equipment soon rolled onto Radio Row, and though some holdouts refused to leave while they tried other legal angles, eventually all of Radio Row was demolished to make room for the World Trade Center.

Posing with a model of Lower Manhattan, architect Minoru Yamasaki points to the future location of the World Trade Center.

creating an interesting and varied interplay of angles and shapes meant to keep the observer's interest. However, the design fell 2 million square feet short of the 10-million-square-foot space requirements of the project. Nevertheless, he shared the idea with the general manager of the World Trade Center project, Guy Tozzoli. Tozzoli remembered a memo to the group studying the project several years earlier, in which public relations specialist Lee K. Jaffe wrote, "If you are going to build a great project, you should build the world's tallest building."[7] Realizing that this was not just a way of getting the desired square footage but also making the building a landmark that would guarantee its financial success and thus attract investors, Tozzoli brought back to the Port Authority a new design by Yamasaki. The new design included twin 110-story towers set in a large plaza with concrete and landscaping, along with four smaller buildings, including a hotel. This plan was quickly adopted, and the architectural firm of Emery Roth and Sons was selected to assist Yamasaki in turning his architectural design into reality.

CONFLICTING PURPOSES, CONFLICTING MESSAGES

While the legal, political, and architectural challenges to the World Trade Center were resolved, a new set of public relations challenges faced the Port Authority. For several years before construction began, Port Authority executive director Austin Tobin had been delivering two conflicting messages to the public.

AUSTIN TOBIN

For decades, the Port Authority and the name Austin Tobin were nearly synonymous. Austin Tobin joined the Port Authority in 1928, only seven years after its founding, as a young corporate attorney who recently graduated from Columbia Law School. He worked for the Port Authority his entire career until he retired in 1972. Tobin became its director in 1942 and served three decades in that post.

Journalist James Morris described Tobin in the following way, reported by Eric Darton in *Divided We Stand: A Biography of New York's World Trade Center*: "He was a small, solid lawyer, weathered but cherubic, like an American Buddha. His voice was gentle but there was a steeliness to his eye, imperfectly disguised in humor. I had been told that he was one of the most powerful men in New York, and it seemed to me that while he would be a mellow and witty dinner host, he might be an awkward opponent to handle, face to face across a conference table with any flaming issue in between."

Tobin avoided calling media or other attention to himself, and only reluctantly gave interviews or press conferences, except when something relating to Port Authority projects, especially the World Trade Center, was at risk. Then he maneuvered skillfully through whatever the crisis was, strengthening the Port Authority's position and increasing its power and scope in the process. By the time he retired, the staff of the Port Authority had grown from three hundred to more than eighty-five hundred. It had an annual budget of $3 billion (up from $200,000 in 1921) and had the power to issue another billion in bonds for projects it undertook. In honor of Tobin, the World Trade Center plaza was named Austin Tobin Plaza in 1982. Today, it, like the rest of the site, lies buried in rubble. Austin Tobin did not live to see the unimaginable end of his prized project. He died of cancer in 1978.

The first was that the sole purpose of building the World Trade Center was to revive the port of New York by promoting New York as a center of world trade. He had to say this because otherwise there would have been no grounds for the Port Authority to be involved. He was careful not to go too deeply into exactly how the two were connected, though, relying on the fact that the Port Authority did not need public approval for any of its projects and thus he did not have to say more than he wished to.

DAVID AND NELSON ROCKEFELLER

The name Rockefeller is one of the best known in New York. The Rockefellers' renown began early in the twentieth century with John D. Rockefeller, who was the chairman of Standard Oil, the main stockholder in Chase Manhattan Bank, and one of the richest men in America. His son was responsible for building New York's landmark Rockefeller Center, but it is his grandsons Nelson and David who were arguably the most prominent Rockefellers of all.

Nelson, who professed to dislike banking, went into politics. He became governor of New York State and ran unsuccessfully for president of the United States before serving as Richard Nixon's vice president. David, who professed to dislike politics, was responsible for maintaining and enhancing the family fortune as chairman of the Chase Manhattan Bank. Both in reality were politically and financially astute, and they worked together to promote David's ideas for revitalizing Lower Manhattan—and making more Rockefeller money in the process.

David was not simply a shrewd businessman. He was sincere in his love of New York, and his enthusiasm for redevelopment made converts of many skeptics. David founded the Downtown–Lower Manhattan Association in 1956 to promote what soon became nicknamed the Billion Dollar Plan for urban renewal. He took the first risky step with family money that same year, building One Chase Plaza on an entire square block of Lower Manhattan to house the Chase Manhattan Bank. In 1958, Nelson was elected governor of New York, and in that role he made many of the decisions about who would sit on the board of the Port Authority and what direction it would take. Between the two of them, David and Nelson Rockefeller controlled most of the political and financial pieces that would make the World Trade Center possible. In fact, a joke running around the city when the towers were built was that they should be named Nelson and David, so closely associated were the two brothers with the towers' existence on the New York skyline.

He simply insinuated that having a large trade complex right next to the port would somehow link the two and instead focused on the benefits of facilitating interaction between businesses involved in world trade. Tobin also promoted the idea of using the World Trade Center as an exposition site for products and ideas, similar to the medieval fair at Leipzig. He pointed out that World's Fairs had been held every few years for several months in various cities, including New York in 1964. He argued that the benefits to business of such fairs could be made more reliable and ongoing by housing a permanent exposition space at the World Trade Center.

The second message was that the World Trade Center would increase the value of downtown property. According to Eric Darton, "Tobin had . . . openly spoken the World Trade Center's secret name. In so doing, [he] went on public record endorsing a speculative real estate venture as the highest form of public good."[8] Time would reveal that the glowing words about using the World Trade Center to revitalize the port were just for show. In fact, many of the piers along the Hudson would quickly be buried under landfill carted away from the World Trade Center excavation, and in time the Port Authority would admit that it had no intention of building a rail tunnel into Manhattan to deliver goods directly to ships. Soon, the Port Authority openly began discussing diverting more and more port activity to New Jersey. The New York City port, the claimed beneficiary of the World Trade Center, would instead become one of its victims.

3

GOING DOWN: PREPARING TO BUILD

When size and location, the last obstacles to going ahead with the World Trade Center project, had been resolved after more than five years of discussion and debate, the equally difficult problem of building it was just beginning. Constructing a skyscraper is difficult under any circumstances, but the location of the World Trade Center, in the middle of an area already densely packed with buildings and people, made the project even more complex. Adding to the complications was the fact that, in many respects, the site was not well suited geologically to construction of such size. Politics and personalities had been formidable adversaries for Austin Tobin and the Port Authority, but they were determined not to be defeated by any opponent, including the existing city or even the land it sat on.

DEMOLITION

The first order of business was clearing the sixteen-acre area—bounded by Vesey Street to the north, Church Street to the east, Liberty Street to the south, and West Street to the west—that would house the World Trade Center. This began on March 21, 1966, when a wrecking crew from the Ajax Wrecking and Lumber Company pulled up in front of 78 Dey Street with sledgehammers and crowbars. The century-old, five-story red brick building at that address had formerly housed a business that sold equipment and goods needed on ships, ironically the kind of business the World Trade Center was supposed to support. Ajax felled the building quickly, then moved on to demolish six others. Although some of the businesses in and around Radio Row were still mounting legal challenges to their evictions, wrecking balls began slamming into empty buildings while holdout merchants tried to carry on business a few doors away. All told, twenty-six buildings in the area were already vacant and were quickly demolished. The rest would follow in time.

Once the area was cleared, new problems arose. Just beneath the World Trade Center site was, according to author Angus Kress Gillespie, "a maze of only partly mapped pipes and cables, forgotten foundations and tunnels, underground streams

The building site of the World Trade Center. Buildings have been demolished and site preparation has begun to make way for the huge complex.

and old graves,"[9] and it was often difficult and time-consuming to determine what had to stay and what needed to be shoveled up and carted away. Furthermore, Manhattan utilities are all located underground, and great care had to be taken not to disrupt the phone, water, electric, gas, and sewer lines that ran under the site.

REMOVAL

The rubble produced from a demolished building is massive and difficult to move, but it is only the first phase of removal. The pit that would have to be dug to accommodate the foundations and basement floors of the World Trade Center would be a far more daunting challenge. How, in the middle of a bustling city, could more than 1.2 million cubic yards of dirt, rock, and other material be carted away? And where could it be taken? According to Gillespie, "Normally the builder would have to take the excavated material away to landfills in New Jersey or dump it way out at sea. By anyone's calculations, that would have been terribly expensive, [requiring] 100,000 truckloads."[10] Actually, Austin Tobin and others had recognized this problem in advance and had turned it to their advantage in their dealings with the city. Lower Manhattan, which is some of the most valuable real estate in the world, could actually become bigger if excavated dirt were used as landfill at the existing waterline. More Manhattan meant more space for buildings and businesses, and thus more taxes for the city treasury.

As part of the approval process for the World Trade Center, a deal had been struck that six square blocks of landfill be created north of an existing public park on the southwest tip of Manhattan. This area, known as Battery Park, is named after a historic fort, or battery, on the site. The new landfill was to be called Battery Park City. Thus both the skyline and the shoreline of New York would be distinctly different as a result of the Port Authority's ambitious project, and the city would gain tax revenues on what was calculated at the time to be $90 million worth of new land for commercial and residential use.

STAYING DRY

The Port Authority, however, was not the first to consider the idea of taking dirt and materials from one part of Manhattan to another to facilitate economic growth. In fact, the actual geological

BATTERY PARK CITY

As part of the agreement regarding the World Trade Center, the Port Authority provided partial compensation to the city of New York for the loss of tax revenues. The agreement also included the construction of new land on the west side of Manhattan. This land, known as Battery Park City, was constructed at the site of old piers and ferry slips, which first had to be torn from their moorings, taken twelve miles out to sea and burned. Then, three-sided boxes called cofferdams, constructed from eighty-five hundred tons of steel, were placed at the outer edges of the future landfill. Each cofferdam was sixty-three feet in diameter, and as it was completed it was filled with six thousand feet, seven barge-loads, of sand. When the entire area was enclosed, the process of filling in the proposed new acreage could begin. All in all, twenty-three new acres of land, $90 million worth at the time, were created.

The land became the most valuable real estate venture undertaken by the city of New York. Apartments and residences there, many with spectacular views of the Statue of Liberty and New York harbor, are among the most expensive in the city. Restaurants and high-priced shops abound, and a marina allows for docking private boats. The World Financial Center houses many major corporations, and was linked to the adjacent World Trade Center by pedestrian bridges. But a full third of Battery Park is open, public space, including a park named for former mayor Robert F. Wagner Jr., who negotiated favorable terms for the city when the World Trade Center sought approvals in the 1960s.

landmass of Manhattan ended right at the site of the World Trade Center. Garbage, wrecked boats and piers, construction fill, and other discarded materials had been dumped at the lower end of Manhattan for centuries, building up the total size of the peninsula. The land at the tip of Lower Manhattan is only approximately three feet above sea level, but bedrock below the World Trade Center site was sixty-five feet down, covered by this man-made fill. Because it was necessary to build on bedrock to ensure the stability of buildings the height and overall size of the Twin

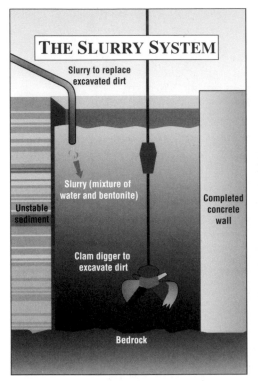

THE SLURRY SYSTEM

Slurry to replace
excavated dirt

Slurry (mixture of
water and bentonite)

Unstable
sediment

Completed
concrete
wall

Clam digger to
excavate dirt

Bedrock

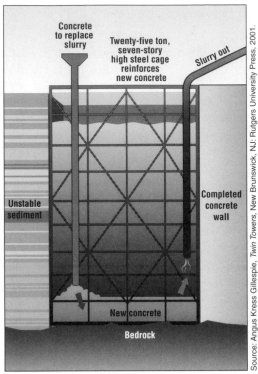

Concrete
to replace
slurry

Twenty-five ton,
seven-story
high steel cage
reinforces
new concrete

Slurry out

Unstable
sediment

Completed
concrete
wall

New concrete

Bedrock

Source: Angus Kress Gillespie, *Twin Towers*, New Brunswick, NJ: Rutgers University Press, 2001.

Towers, the excavation for the project would have to be very deep. However, engineers knew that the holes would begin to fill and cave in when the water level was reached only a few feet down.

Several options were considered, including developing a way of continually pumping the water out of the excavation. But studies showed that any large-scale pumping effort would undermine the foundations of nearby buildings, perhaps leading to their collapse. Furthermore, there were concerns about what could be long-term problems with flooding and seepage even after construction was complete.

The solution was a gamble proposed by Port Authority chief engineer John M. Kyle that involved an unusual building technique known as the slurry trench. The slurry trench had been perfected in Europe for subway construction in low-lying areas and used widely in drilling oil wells, but it had never been applied to building foundations. The slurry used was a mix of water and a natural clay called bentonite. Bentonite absorbs large amounts of water, and swells up to create a thick, souplike mixture that is strong enough to keep a hole from collapsing or filling with water.

Digging was accomplished with clam diggers, clawlike devices that closed to form buckets at the end of long mechanical arms. As sections three feet wide by twenty-two feet long were dug, slurry replaced the dirt being excavated. When bedrock was reached, a twenty-five-ton, seven-story-high steel cage was lowered into the slurry. This cage would serve to reinforce the concrete that was then poured around it in the slurry-filled pit. The concrete forced the slurry up and out of the hole, where it was reclaimed and used for the next section of excavation.

OLD SHOES AND SHIP TIMBERS

Any time a major excavation takes place in a location with a long human history, conflicts arise between those who want to get the project done efficiently and those who want to take advantage of the excavation to discover interesting artifacts that can help people understand the past. Archaeologists in New York were interested in preserving whatever could be salvaged, a desire that prompted Construction Manager Ray Monti, quoted in Angus Kress Gillespie's *Twin Towers*, to say that they wanted to excavate the site "with spoons."

What happened was a compromise. Durable objects that could be seen were salvaged, including a set of tools that was reported missing by a worker, Charlie Schmidt, in 1904. A time capsule buried in 1884 was the most interesting find. It had been buried by local merchants and included business cards, an opera playbill, and election flyers featuring Grover Cleveland. Despite the clumsiness of the excavation equipment and the speed of the work, many smaller items were recovered, including drinking glasses, clay pipes, bottles, and coins. An old shoe, made to fit either foot, was also found. It could be dated to 1865 or earlier, when shoes began to be designed differently for left and right feet. Nautical items were also located, including old anchors, but not the remains of a ship of historic interest, the *Tiger*, a trading vessel that had caught on fire and sank near the World Trade Center site in 1613. Hopes were high that it could be located, but no trace of it was found.

A rectangle two city blocks long and four blocks wide, made of 152 of these reinforced concrete panels reaching to bedrock, was constructed, forming what was widely referred to as a "reverse bathtub." Although the bathtub was not part of the actual structure, its purpose was to keep water permanently out of the site. It worked brilliantly, and is often cited as one of the techno-

DUST AND DISRUPTION

For the duration of the construction of the World Trade Center, traffic patterns were disrupted in much of Lower Manhattan. Some streets were obliterated altogether by the project. Traffic that normally would have flowed through the site now had to be diverted around it, adding to the congestion on the remaining streets. Pedestrian traffic was also diverted around the site, making mob scenes of sidewalks and crosswalks in the immediate area.

Other related problems occurred as well. Many of the delis, cafés, and restaurants where workers bought lunch had been demolished, and those that remained were more crowded than ever. Even in expensive restaurants, waiters tried to rush people in and out in a half hour, after they had already waited equally long just to be seated. And customers were easily irritated by anyone who arrived at the front of a fast-food line with a question or a dilemma about what to order. Those who decided to forgo lines for food found themselves unwelcome as browsers in stores, because stores often became so crowded it was difficult to serve paying customers.

Some shop owners faced more difficult problems than crowds, however. The noise, dust, and fumes from construction made working near the site a nightmare. One owner of a pet store lost much of his stock of birds, monkeys, puppies, and other animals because they were so upset by the noise they went into convulsions, banged their heads against their cages, aborted fetuses, and otherwise harmed themselves. But the worst problem befell businesses on nearby Liberty Street. There, in April 1968, the prolonged percussion caused by the excavation of the World Trade Center site caused the collapse of a stretch of the whole street.

logical innovations that made the World Trade Center possible. The bathtub took fourteen months of nearly twenty-four-hour-a-day work to complete. But once finished, the construction of the actual towers and the rest of the World Trade Center could take place in a dry space. The excavation for the World Trade Center also had no negative effect on the water table underneath other buildings in Manhattan.

KEEPING THE CITY MOVING

All of the buildings in Lower Manhattan made it a bustling place even before the World Trade Center was built. There, residents went about their daily lives, living in homes ranging from the tenements that had housed various immigrant groups for the past century to Greenwich Village's quirky mix of historic buildings converted to luxury residences and digs for students from nearby New York University. But residents were a minority in Lower Manhattan. It was during the regular workweek that the population swelled with workers who lived across the Hudson River in New Jersey or in Brooklyn, the Bronx, Queens, or Staten Island, the other four boroughs making up New York City.

A great deal of foot, automobile, and bus traffic had to be diverted around the huge construction site for the World Trade Center, but the bigger problem lay underground. Most New Yorkers did not walk to work, and even fewer attempted to drive the congested, gridlocked streets. Many took the bus, but typically a New Yorker made the commute all or in part by subway trains. Commuters living in New Jersey would enter a train tunnel on the New Jersey side of the Hudson, then proceed underwater across the river. Reaching land on the other side, the train continued underground, stopping at stations deep below the earth. There, passengers would alight and take escalators to the busy streets outside.

The Hudson and Manhattan Commuter Railroad, officially renamed the Port Authority Trans-Hudson line, or PATH, was one such subway line linking New Jersey on the other side of the river to Lower Manhattan. The PATH tunnels ran directly through the construction site and could not be rerouted because their new terminal was to be at the World Trade Center. The workers would have to excavate around them, but the old iron tunnels inside which the trains ran would collapse once the earth underneath them was removed. The subway tunnels were eighteen feet above bedrock, so when the excavation reached them, an elaborate system of metal and wood scaffolding was erected to support the tunnels. Saw cuts were made in the tubes to allow for contraction and expansion of the newly exposed metal, a matter of no concern when the tubes were buried but a very real problem in the extreme air temperatures of New York City. One PATH conductor was so unnerved the first time he saw a thin slice of sunlight across the tracks created by the new saw cut that he slammed on the brakes in a panic, thinking that a huge disaster must have occurred. According to Angus Gillespie, protective strips were soon placed over the cuts "to allow the trains to roll along through the same gloom"[11] as always. Throughout the construction, passengers were unaware at what point they passed through the building site because there were no windows in the tubes. They continued to travel in total darkness until they disembarked into the chaos of construction in Lower Manhattan.

FOUNDATIONS AND FOOTINGS

Once the subway had been adequately cradled, attention could turn to pouring the foundation. Almost two and a half years after wreckers had shown up on Dey Street to demolish the first of the former buildings on the site, huge reinforced concrete base pads were poured onto the bedrock. Onto these base pads were placed steel cages known as grillages. A grillage is a heavy-duty frame of crisscrossed steel beams that is used to distribute the weight of extremely heavy loads over as wide an area as possible. To reinforce the grillages, each of which weighed thirty-four tons and was fifteen feet long by eleven feet wide by seven feet high, steel base plates were placed along the exterior walls of the grillage and mounted directly, as were the grillages, onto the concrete pad below. These base plates, each between seven and nine square feet and six to ten inches thick, weighed between four and twelve tons. Altogether, twenty-eight such concrete bases and reinforced grillages were needed to support each tower.

To builders, the transition between foundation work and construction work occurs at the moment the first structure is placed onto the foundation slabs. Therefore, Wednesday, August 6, 1968, was a day etched in the minds of Ray Monti, the project's construction manager, and Karl Koch, the man whose

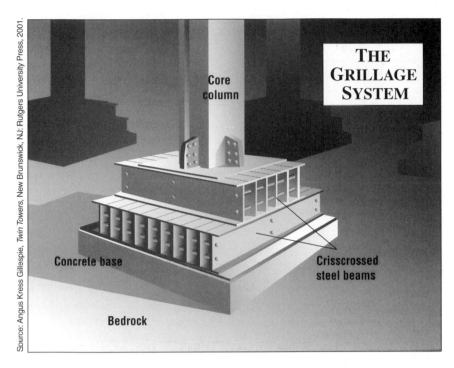

THE GRILLAGE SYSTEM

Core column

Concrete base

Crisscrossed steel beams

Bedrock

company had won a more than $20 million contract to assemble all the steelwork for the project. On that day, the first grillage was guided into place by a team of workers and set down onto its slab at the southwest corner of the north tower. Construction had begun on the tallest buildings in the world.

4

SOLVING THE PROBLEMS OF SIZE

The huge pit and concrete bases from which metal pillars had begun to sprout at the World Trade Center site looked like the beginnings of any skyscraper. But this was not to be just any other building. The blueprints for 110 stories showed that clearly. Though they would not be the world's tallest buildings for long—the slightly taller Sears Tower in Chicago was scheduled for completion in approximately a year—the Twin Towers would remain the tallest twin buildings in the world, and the tallest structures in one of the most glamorous cities in the world. Buildings that later surpassed the World Trade Center in height could not surpass it in the public eye. Few modern buildings in the world had greater name recognition or more visual familiarity than the two towers jutting out above the other skyscrapers in Lower Manhattan. Height adds complications, however, and even though Minoru Yamasaki's solutions received scant architectural praise, they did produce some major innovations in design, many of which are still widely used today.

BEARING THE WEIGHT

To the untrained eye, the huge building going up in Lower Manhattan in the late 1960s might have looked like any other. However, those with an interest in building construction would quickly have noticed how unusual it was. Before the World Trade Center, tall buildings were normally constructed in a manner somewhat like building a tower out of many dining room tables. The weight of the floors was borne by many small pillars (the legs of the tables) more or less evenly spaced throughout the interior. The exterior walls, what people saw from the outside, in modern high rises were what architects call "curtain walls." Curtain walls do not bear any weight; they function solely to close in the interior space of the building. It is precisely because they do not bear the weight of the building that they can be made of glass, as they are on many modern buildings.

The Twin Towers would be radically different. Support for each building was to come from two different elements, exterior walls and approximately forty supporting columns, clustered together in the center of the tower. Around this central core, each

The core columns, an important structural element in the Twin Towers, are visible in this photograph.

MINORU YAMASAKI

The architect of the World Trade Center, Minoru Ya-masaki, was the son of Japanese immigrants. Yamasaki was born in Seattle, where his father was on the mainte-nance crew for a shoe factory, in 1912. Yamasaki grew up in a culture hostile to Asian immigrants. During his child-hood, he was forbidden to swim in the public pool or sit anywhere but the balcony of movie theaters. When he en-tered the University of Washington, he paid his tuition and expenses by working hundred-hour weeks during the summer in Alaskan fish canneries. After earning architec-ture degrees at the University of Washington and New York University, he worked for many years as a junior ar-chitect in various firms before being successful enough to launch his own firm in Detroit. The firm quickly grew to more than fifty employees and relocated to the same posh suburb where fifteen years before, upon his arrival in De-troit, a real estate agent had refused to sell him a home.

Success took a heavy toll on Yamasaki. His marriage disintegrated, he developed bleeding ulcers, and he strug-gled with a morphine addiction acquired while hospitalized on several occasions. According to Eric Darton, author of *Di-vided We Stand: A Biography of New York's World Trade Center*, "No setback slowed Yamasaki down for long, though, and with dozens of workmanlike, solidly engi-neered—and increasingly vertical—projects under his belt, he had, through sheer force of will, attained a position where he could successfully compete against the forty other architects who submitted proposals to design the WTC."

Yamasaki, or Yama, as he was called by his friends, stood just over five feet tall. Nevertheless, by virtue of his design for the World Trade Center, controversial as it was, he became a giant in twentieth-century American archi-tecture. He died on February 7, 1986.

floor had a full acre of open space with no other interruptions. This would dramatically increase the square footage of each floor that could be made available for rent, and would make vir-tually any configuration of interior space possible. For this to be a workable design, the weight of the building, which would conventionally have been borne by the many interior pillars, would have to be displaced outward to the skeleton and inward to the core.

Such a design would not have been possible when many of New York's other famous skyscrapers were built because the high-strength steel it required was not available. This type of steel was more expensive but necessary, particularly for the exterior walls. To support the weight of the building, there would need to be many columns of this special steel running the entire height of the structure, spaced a little under four feet apart.

The exterior of the World Trade Center required massive amounts of steel to insure structural integrity.

This structural requirement is what would give the World Trade Center its unique—and controversial—appearance. The windows would each be only twenty-two inches wide, totaling a relatively small 30 percent of the exterior. The windows would be even less prominent because they were to be recessed, meaning the windows would be mounted three-quarters of the way back from the outer edge of the steel columns, making the façade look like a single, solid piece of ridged metal, totally unlike the solid glass exteriors of the "international style" that was so popular at the time. Author and professor Angus Kress Gillespie compared the design to "two stalks of celery."[12] The eventual appearance of the building gave it a sense of solidity and mass that some felt should have been avoided in such a huge structure. Glass reflects the sky and thus seems less intrusive and overwhelming. The reflections of light off the World Trade Center were far subtler, a lustrous glow changing hue as the day progressed.

WITHSTANDING THE WEATHER

The solid exterior of the World Trade Center would have another purpose as well. Wind becomes an increasing factor as buildings rise. In fact, from approximately the thirtieth floor upward, accommodating the lateral, or sideways, forces of wind is as much of a consideration as supporting the building's weight. Buildings that sway too much may collapse, and even if they did not, the people inside would be unable to work because they would experience nausea and other symptoms associated with motion sickness. The World Trade Center's exterior skeleton made the buildings extremely rigid, capable of withstanding sustained winds of 150 miles per hour—stronger than any wind ever recorded in New York history—without moving laterally more than three feet, well within the safety zone for its occupants. Likely movement would be far less, which would add to the occupants' sense of comfort. To withstand maximum winds, special glass eight times stronger than average would be used in the windows, so even the severe storms that occasionally strike Manhattan would pose no risk to occupants of the towers.

Claims about the strength of the outer walls were often, and now eerily, tied to improbable scenarios. Simulations in wind tunnels showed that the towers could withstand 13 million pounds of pressure from the outside, which one observer pointed out meant that it could survive being hit head on by an ocean liner. In fact, the possibility of the towers being hit by a plane had been considered, and it had been calculated that the towers would not collapse if this happened. Of course, what people had in mind was a 1970s-size commercial aircraft, considerably smaller than many in use today, ramming the building by accident, not a large aircraft fully loaded with explosive jet fuel.

Each tower was to be supported not just by the exterior columns but at the center by its core columns. The core would be large, but it would also include the shafts for all the elevators, another way in which rentable office space was maximized. The core columns were designed to support 60 percent of the building's weight, while the exterior walls would support the other 40 percent. Each tower would have four core columns, each a slightly different overall shape due to the dimensions of the different elevator systems.

GETTING UP AND DOWN

Although withstanding wind is a major design requirement for tall buildings, without another innovation, buildings could never

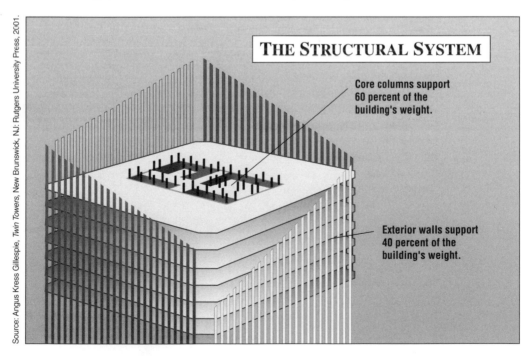

THE STRUCTURAL SYSTEM

Core columns support 60 percent of the building's weight.

Exterior walls support 40 percent of the building's weight.

Source: Angus Kress Gillespie, *Twin Towers*, New Brunswick, NJ: Rutgers University Press, 2001.

have risen high enough for wind to be a factor. That innovation is the elevator. Before elevators were invented, the height of a building was limited to how many flights of stairs a person could reasonably travel on foot. The value of office space declined with every floor a person had to climb, giving builders little incentive to incur the extra costs of additional stories. Buildings rarely went even as high as eight floors until the Tower and Equitable Buildings were constructed with the first mechanical elevators. In a building with an elevator, it does not really matter whether an office is located on the second, twenty-second, or fifty-second floor. So after the elevator became a standard part of new buildings,

OBSERVING THE CONSTRUCTION

Although public relations might have seemed like a minor problem compared to figuring out how to make 110-story buildings sturdy and usable, the Port Authority continually faced public resistance and resentment, especially as the actual construction began disrupting lives in Lower Manhattan. One of the things the Port Authority did in an attempt to bolster support for the project among the business community it hoped to attract was open a visitors' reception area on the seventeenth floor of a nearby building. The facility had a clear view down into the construction site, and was equipped with big viewing windows for visitors and for television crews filming stories about the project. The views were so expansive that steel could be seen being taken off barges, landfill could be observed going into Battery Park City, and Radio Row could be witnessed being demolished. The center included a room equipped for presentations as well as an area containing a scale model of the project, photographs, and other promotional material.

The visitors' reception area was not open to the public. Instead, during the months of the year when weather permitted, ordinary workers and residents of Lower Manhattan could go up on ten-foot-high platforms at each end of the construction site and look down at the work going on. Specially uniformed and attractive young women trained to answer a wide range of questions about architecture, engineering, and construction staffed these platforms.

architects began to design taller buildings. What kept the height limits on most buildings lower than they technologically could have been was the fact that elevator shafts take up so much room in a building. The higher the building, the more space there is to rent. The more space there is to rent, the more people will work and do business in the building. The more people in the building, the more elevators will be needed. It simply was not cost effective to keep building higher and higher.

A Grand Scheme

Figuring out a scheme for the World Trade Center elevators that would not end up taking away all the space gained by Yamasaki's innovative design proved elusive for the World Trade Center architects in the early stages of building design. One day, one of the architects had an inspiration when he was riding the New York subway. People who take the subway often cannot get to their destination without changing trains at least once. Why, architect Herb Tessler reasoned, couldn't the World Trade Center use the same principle in designing its elevator system? Not all elevators had to start on the ground floor, or go all the way to the top. Tessler proposed building three sets of passenger elevators in addition to the nine freight elevators in the building plans. The first set would be express elevators that went all the way to the top of the towers to serve what would be the viewing platform on one tower and the Windows on the World restaurant on the other. These would be the equivalent of a subway ride directly to one's destination. Because people are not aware of the speed they are traveling but only the speed at which they are accelerating and decelerating, formulas were worked out to minimize the discomfort of using the express elevators, yet allow them to go sixteen hundred feet a minute rather than the conventional eight hundred to twelve hundred.

The second set of elevators Tessler proposed involved dividing the building into three zones. In addition to the ground-floor lobby, there would be another lobby at the forty-fourth floor, and a third lobby at the seventy-eighth floor. One group of express elevators would start on the ground floor and, traveling as quickly as human comfort allowed, go straight to the first "sky lobby" and stop there. Another group would go directly to the second sky lobby.

The third set of elevators would be local ones, operating from the ground floor and the two sky lobbies. If a person had to

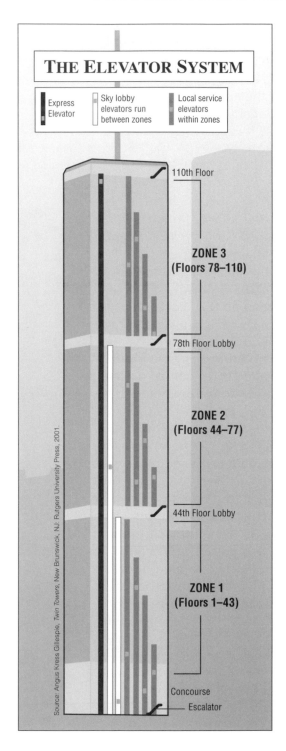

THE ELEVATOR SYSTEM

Express Elevator

Sky lobby elevators run between zones

Local service elevators within zones

110th Floor

ZONE 3
(Floors 78–110)

78th Floor Lobby

ZONE 2
(Floors 44–77)

44th Floor Lobby

ZONE 1
(Floors 1–43)

Concourse

Escalator

Source: Angus Kress Gillespie, *Twin Towers*, New Brunswick, NJ: Rutgers University Press, 2001.

go to the thirty-sixth floor, for example, the local elevators on the ground floor would meet that need. If someone needed to get to the fifty-second floor, he or she would take the express directly to the first sky lobby, then take a local elevator from there. If the destination were the eighty-fifth floor, the second group of express elevators would take the person directly to the seventy-eighth floor sky lobby, where a local elevator would complete the journey. For those who would have only a floor or two to go from the lobby, escalators would be added for their convenience.

The advantage to this plan was that one set of shafts could be used for all the local elevators. For example, the local elevator for the first zone would terminate at the forty-third floor. Another car would start on the forty-fourth floor in the same elevator shaft that went to the seventy-seventh floor, and a third car served the floors above the second sky lobby. This would maximize the use of each elevator shaft and make it possible to have fewer shafts overall.

One final innovation pioneered at the World Trade Center was the entry and exit procedure for passengers. The elevators, eventually designed by Otis Elevator Company, would hold up to fifty-five people and were designed so that people entered through doors on one side of the car and got off through a second set of doors on the other side. This would speed up boarding and getting off because people more or less remained lined up as they were when they got on, rather than jockeying for position or squeezing into corners to make room.

Tessler's idea was originally not well received by key advisers on the project. Many felt that people would not want to change elevators and that it would therefore be difficult to get people to rent space in the upper floors. However, supporters of the idea argued that, due to the size and speed of the elevators and the efficiency of the zone system, the trip to the upper floors would actually be much faster than by conventional systems, even after factoring in the time required to exit the first elevator, cross the sky lobby, and wait for a second elevator. Even on the lower floors, the elevators would be extremely fast, reaching the

THE REST OF THE WORLD TRADE CENTER

Although the Twin Towers captured most of the attention at the World Trade Center, they were in fact only the centerpiece of a much bigger architectural plan. The entire project consisted of the towers, a five-square-acre plaza, and four much smaller buildings. The project was designed as a single artistic composition, using color and shape to create unity and interest. The plaza pavement was a grayish marble, at the center of which was a fountain and a globe-shaped sculpture by Fritz Koenig. White lines on the plaza pavement converged at the fountain to draw the viewer's attention inward to the center of the plaza. Flower boxes added color to the fountain area, which also had benches for people to sit on to view the towers or the people passing by. Two other sculptures were showcased on the plaza, one in stainless steel by James Rosati, and the other a black granite composition by Masayuki Nagare. The towers rose at the south and west corners of the plaza. On the other sides were four other buildings, clad in brownish aluminum to contrast with the towers, including a Marriott hotel, the United States Customs Building, and two other office buildings. All were destroyed or heavily damaged on September 11, 2001.

fortieth floor in less than half a minute. Eventually, these arguments prevailed and Tessler's sky-lobby system (now widely imitated) was given the go-ahead. Altogether, twenty-three express elevators to the sky lobbies and seventy-two local elevators would be constructed. The buildings would actually have more elevator capacity than computer formulas said was needed, but nevertheless each floor still had 75 percent of its space available for rental, far exceeding the 62 percent that had been the top figure achieved by previous skyscraper designs.

Once the major problems associated with constructing the world's tallest buildings had been resolved, blueprints and other plans for the actual construction of the towers could be finalized. Critical details, such as the specific weight-bearing requirements for the foundation pillars, were checked and rechecked. But for the architects, engineers, and others involved in the project, it was an exhilarating time. They knew now for certain that they would be part of an architectural triumph, perhaps the greatest they would ever know. The tallest buildings in the world would soon rise, the product of their collective imagination and intelligence.

5

GOING UP: CONSTRUCTION AND COMPLICATIONS

Constructing a building complex as massive as the World Trade Center is, in some respects, like waging a war. In fact, Construction Manager Ray Monti once described the process as "like the D-Day invasion in terms of the intricacy of planning and coordination."[13] It seemed as if every stage presented something new to battle with. First, there were the problems associated with getting construction materials in almost unimaginable quantities to the site, including 192,000 tons of steel, 1,520 miles of wire, and 7 million square feet of acoustical ceiling tiles the buildings would require. Then there were problems associated with maintaining adequate working conditions for the laborers, problems that more than once caused the workers' unions to intervene. Labor slowdowns and even strikes added to the already difficult task of keeping construction moving along. Although the towers inched steadily into the sky above Manhattan, there must have been many times when those involved wondered if the project would ever get finished.

STEEL AND MORE STEEL

The complications created both by people and by the need for materials in such massive amounts had been apparent early on. Arrangements to buy the needed steel had been undertaken well in advance of the completed plans for the building. There was no point in waiting because it was clear that whatever the exact amount of steel needed would be, it was going to be close to 200,000 tons. U.S. Steel and Bethlehem Steel, the two largest manufacturers in the country, had been solicited to supply the steel, but toward the end of the negotiating process they suddenly and without warning adjusted their bids upward by half, angering the Port Authority negotiators.

The Port Authority responded by deciding not to go with these two suppliers and instead contract with fifteen smaller companies to supply all the required steel. This ended up being a far better arrangement. The combined bill for the steel from all fifteen smaller companies came to $85.4 million; the combined bids from U.S. Steel and Bethlehem Steel had totaled in excess of $240 million. The downside of this arrangement was that dealing with fifteen suppliers was more complicated. To make the process more efficient, the Port Authority enlisted a "middleman," a contractor responsible for the installation of all the steel supplied by the other companies. Karl Koch Erecting Company was awarded the contract to receive, perform quality controls on, and install all steel the World Trade Center would require.

GETTING THE PIECES RIGHT

Once it was clear that the materials would be available, a new set of complications arose. Whether one is simply preparing to

During the bidding to supply steel for the huge World Trade Center project, Bethlehem Steel (pictured) and U.S. Steel became greedy. They raised their bids unreasonably and were rejected by the Port Authority as suppliers.

build or already raising a building, materials need to be transported not only away from the construction site but also to it. The problem of getting landfill and debris from the construction site had been solved by the creation of Battery Park City. Now, one of the most vexing problems facing the construction managers and contractors was the lack of a place to keep materials that had to be brought to the site. Manhattan is crammed with buildings, and it was already greatly impacted by the barricading off of the sixteen-acre construction site. There was no way any more space could be given over for the project.

One hundred acres of an old railroad yard across the Hudson River in Greenville, New Jersey, was converted into a storage area for the steel needed for the World Trade Center. Ironically, the reason the yard had lain idle was the shift from railroad to real estate interests of the wealthy of New York, the very shift that was bringing the World Trade Center to reality. Various methods of transportation for the ten miles between the Greenville yard and the construction site were used, including trucks and boats and even, at one point, a helicopter. For the most part, pieces small enough to be transported by flatbed truck were brought over through the Holland Tunnel in the predawn hours when traffic was light. Larger pieces were brought across the river in barges propelled by tugboats.

Space constraints made it particularly important for materials to be ready to be installed quickly upon arrival at the site. There was not enough room for unused materials to be stored there for long. To address this situation, some pieces of the building were preconstructed off-site. If it was feasible, for example, to weld or bolt together smaller pieces, and then bring the assembled parts across the river for installation, this method was preferred over doing the welding and bolting at the construction site.

Preconstruction saved some time and space, but massive buildings are made up largely of heavy steel beams, and getting these to the site just before they were to be installed was of equal importance. If a particular beam was not available when needed, the work schedules not only of the steelworkers installing it but also of the crane operators, welders, riveters, and others doing tasks related to it would be affected. Costs would mount and deadlines would be missed. Therefore, an elaborate system for marking and identifying materials was needed so that trucks would head off from Greenville with only the materials needed right at the moment. This system, informally referred to as the just-in-time method, required remarkable organization.

In the Greenville yard, an area more than ten square city blocks had been filled with rows of steel parts, some weighing over fifty tons. Each piece was stenciled with a long series of numbers and letters that the trained observer could quickly de-

Preconstruction and the "just-in-time" system allowed materials to be delivered to the building site efficiently.

code. Angus Gillespie in *Twin Towers*, offers one such number, PONYA WTC 213.00 236B 4-9 558 35 TONS, as an example. The first series of letters identifies the beam on which this number was stenciled as destined for the Port of New York Authority's World Trade Center project, contract number 213.00. According to Gillespie, this beam had its own individual number, 236B, "and it was to be used between floors four and nine. The derrick division number was 558, which determined which crane would lift it onto the building and the order in which it was to be erected."[14]

This system was very effective, resulting in the movement of more than thirty truckloads of steel a day, each averaging eighteen tons of materials. The goal, which was often achieved, was to deliver materials within a half hour of their scheduled delivery time. This enabled an average of six hundred tons of steel to be added to the building each day.

LABOR PROBLEMS

Despite the many creative solutions to make the construction of the World Trade Center as efficient as possible, all did not go smoothly at the beginning stages. Workers on the World Trade Center site were union members, and from the beginning, their respective unions looked out for their best interests. During the course of the construction, several labor disputes caused tension between the unions and the Port Authority. The most serious of these developed into strikes by tugboat and elevator workers.

The first major strike, that of the tugboat pilots, seriously affected the flow of materials to the construction site because the materials had to be brought across the Hudson River by barges pushed and steered by tugboats. The tugboat strike is notable because of the Port Authority construction manager's efforts to keep working despite the strike. Using a "sky crane," a helicopter used to carry heavy loads of up to ten tons by air, attempts were made to fly floor panels across the river to the construction site. The first panel met with wind resistance and began to swing, causing the helicopter pilot to ditch the huge piece of metal into the Hudson River, where it remains today. Even though the attempt was made early on a Saturday morning when traffic was minimal, many people saw the drop and were upset by what clearly had been an unsafe maneuver. Nevertheless, several more unsuccessful attempts were made before

LUNCH HOUR AT THE WORLD TRADE CENTER

On small construction projects, when the lunch hour comes, workers either eat what they have brought from home or dash to a nearby fast-food outlet, trying to eat and get back in a half hour. However, when a high-rise building project reaches a certain level, it could take the entire lunch period just to get down to the ground. Different construction companies have dealt with this problem in different ways, but none at the time had gone as far as at the World Trade Center. There, the Port Authority contracted with a company to feed work crews right on the floors where they were working. The company, American News, used its commissary in Lower Manhattan to prepare food, which was then delivered and reheated on-site with movable equipment. In essence, a temporary restaurant was set up high in the sky, where more than a thousand workers could be served each workday. This benefited the workers and the contractors alike, for the workers got a hot and nutritious meal and were back on the job in thirty minutes.

the idea was abandoned in favor of a roundabout route using regular trucks, which turned a short, direct trip into a journey that took most of the night.

Several other strikes, including that of the teamsters and that of sheet-metal workers, followed, but the most serious was the elevator workers' strike in 1969, which lasted almost four months. At the time, elevator workers were involved in installing the construction elevators serving the towers. During the strike, all laborers had to walk up to and down from their work sites on the towers, which had by then reached twenty-seven stories. The Port Authority also had to figure out ways to get tools and food to the workers without using the most efficient and convenient means, the elevators.

CREATING THE SIGNATURE DESIGN

By the summer of 1969, labor problems had been resolved and, the core of the north tower had risen to the ninth floor, while the steel at the perimeter had reached the fifth floor. It was a critical time. The main decorative, or design, element of the en-

tire building was the narrowing of widely spaced columns at
the entry level to smaller intervals for the remaining stories of
the building. The design was an innovative one, resulting in a
modernistic take on the pointed Gothic arches of medieval
cathedrals. It also made it appear from the outside that the
huge tower was being held up only by the slenderest and most

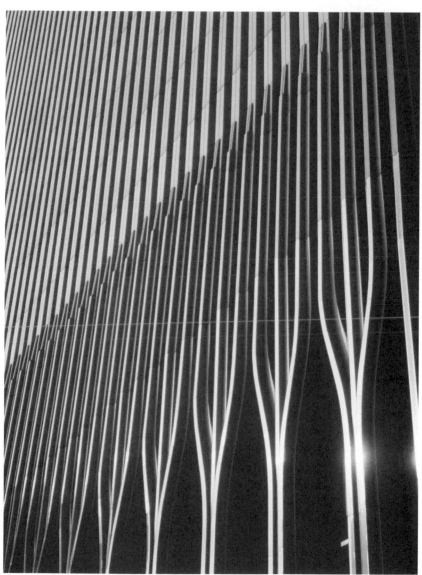

The modern take on medieval Gothic arches became a signature design element of the World Trade Center.

graceful of arched columns. The wider columns at the base were, of course, not only aesthetic but also necessary for people to get in and out of the building. They also allowed for a soaring and spacious interior lobby. However, Minoru Yamasaki deliberately wanted to create the opposite feeling on the upper levels, a feeling that one could not get out or, more accurately, inadvertently fall through the windows.

Special pieces of steel were required to accomplish this design. Fifty-ton columns, each fifty-one feet long, were created roughly in the shape of a wishbone. Each of these was bolted and welded to the entry columns with its two prongs up, enabling three columns to rise out of one, and creating on the underside a pointed Gothic arch. In this fashion, the ten-foot open spaces between columns at the entry level were reduced to three-feet, four-inch intervals for the remaining floors.

STEEL MEETS SKY

Whether assembling a decorative or a structural element of a building, the basic techniques of constructing steel frame buildings are the same, regardless of size. Steel is bolted and welded as required to create a strong structure that can handle both the weight of the building and, in high-rises, external forces such as wind. But height adds complications to the construction process itself. The most notable of these complications is that steel must be delivered to wherever the construction is taking place. As each floor is added, the difficulty of building the next one increases.

The Twin Towers were by no means the first buildings to pose the complications of height. At lower levels, cranes mounted at street level are routinely used to hoist materials, but they usually are limited to floors lower than the height of their movable arm, or boom. They also are not considered very safe because they have toppled over from time to time, causing injury or death as well as property damage. For tall buildings, strong machines known as derricks, capable of lifting extremely heavy weights, were generally used. A drawback of derricks, however, is that they do not operate from the ground but must be situated on the building being constructed. This means that the floors of the building have to be able to withstand the weight of the derrick. (This is comparable to an upper floor of an apartment or house that has to be built strong enough to bear the weight of a car rather than a few people.)

MOHAWKS ON THE TOWERS

"They have high cheekbones and jut noses, their eyes are sad, shrewd and dark brown, their hair is straight and coal black, their skin is smooth and coppery, and they have the same beautiful, chin-lifted, haughty walk that gypsies have." These words of author Joseph Mitchell in his 1949 essay "The Mohawks in High Steel" are quoted by Angus Kress Gillespie in *Twin Towers: The Life of New York City's World Trade Center.* Despite Mitchell's obvious admiration for the demeanor and appearance of the Mohawks, a group of Native Americans, what was most impressive about them to Mitchell and others was their apparently complete lack of fear of heights. This had been noted years before, in 1886, during the construction of a bridge across the St. Lawrence River in Canada, the Mohawks' home. Gillespie quotes from a letter written by the manager of that project:

> These Indians were as agile as goats. They would walk a narrow beam up in the air with nothing below them but the river. . . . They were inquisitive about the riveting and were continually bothering our foremen by requesting that they be allowed to take a crack at it. This happens to be the most dangerous work in all construction, and the highest paid. Men who want to do it are rare and men who can do it even rarer, and . . . there are sometimes not enough of them to go around. We decided it would be mutually advantageous to see what these Indians could do . . . and it turned out that putting riveting tools in their hands was like putting ham with eggs.

Mohawks soon became part of many high-rise construction projects in the United States and Canada, including the World Trade Center. There, twelve of the forty-five riveters were Mohawks, most of them living during the week in Brooklyn and commuting on weekends back to their homes in Canada.

This was not an insurmountable problem, but it added to the difficulty of construction. The bigger problem involved with using derricks is the fact that they have to be moved to upper floors as the building grows. This is difficult to accomplish as well as time-consuming. It takes at least a day and a half to move a derrick one floor up. This process costs money and time, so the builders of the World Trade Center wanted to avoid using derricks if possible.

The alternative to using derricks came from an Australian company that built a machine nicknamed the kangaroo crane. According to Angus Kress Gillespie, at first glance the crane did not look that unusual: "It had a 110-foot boom painted red and white for aircraft safety, a red cab, and a counterweight at the rear. Less ordinary was its mounting. It sat atop a thin steel structure, 12 feet by 12 feet, which was 120 feet high. The lower eighty feet of this tower fitted into the elevator core."[15] Essentially, a kangaroo crane perched atop each tower, one crane at each corner of the elevator core. It was stabilized by a long base wedged deep into the core that functioned, in the words of Austin Tobin, "like a sword in a sheath."[16]

The cranes' booms reached over the edge of the building and were able to pick up steel from the ground and deliver it to the highest levels of the building. With its boom extended sixty feet, a kangaroo crane could lift a fifty-ton piece of metal. This was possible only because of the four eleven-ton counterweights at the other end of the boom, which balanced the heavy weight of the beam being lifted much in the way a seesaw balances its two riders. These machines were so effective at higher levels that they actually created a new set of complications caused by the fact that the crane operator eventually was too high above the ground supervisor to see hand signals. Telephones had to be used to tell the crane operator to rotate the crane, raise or lower the boom, and lift.

The nickname "kangaroo crane" came about not just because it shared its country of origin with those unique animals but because of another similar characteristic they shared. Kangaroo cranes were equipped with motors powering a hydraulic system that functioned similarly to those used in auto shops to lift cars. When the crane had lifted all the materials needed for the topmost three floors of a building under construction, it could lift itself up the elevator shaft to a new level, twelve feet at a "jump." What took almost two days with a derrick took only about two hours with a kangaroo crane.

THE PIECES COME TOGETHER

With the just-in-time delivery method running smoothly for the most part, and the kangaroo cranes in place to lift materials to where they were needed, construction could move ahead quickly. It proceeded in a similar manner for the entire

Kangaroo cranes, pictured here, proved invaluable during the construction of the towers.

GETTING THE KANGAROO CRANES DOWN

Kangaroo cranes could "jump" only one way: up. After the towers topped out, the cranes sat atop the elevator shafts, posing a problem for the Port Authority construction managers. There was only one solution. One crane was dismantled and lowered directly to the ground by another crane. However, that left one final crane stranded high in the sky, unable, of course, to lower itself. To solve this problem, a derrick was hoisted up to the roof by the last crane. The derrick then lowered pieces of the dismantled crane to the ground. Workers then took the derrick apart into pieces small enough to take to the ground by freight elevator.

construction process. First, a few floors of the core were constructed. While this was going on, the exterior wall was built to the same height. The exterior wall was made from prefabricated grids of vertical columns welded to spandrels, or horizontal beams. These panels were two or three stories high, and each weighed over twenty tons.

Next, the floor was installed. The floor supports were thirty-two-inch-deep trusses, or triangular frames. These trusses had a special lip on the top that functioned like a shallow pan to hold the concrete that was poured to make the floor. In the space below the poured concrete, there was plenty of room to mount phone and power lines as well as the air conditioning and plumbing systems. Because the floor is also the ceiling for the story below it, the last step was to mount ceiling tiles at the bottom of the trusses. On any given day, construction workers on the site were joined by dozens or even hundreds of electricians, tilers, and others doing specialized tasks to turn the building frame into a completed project.

The final step in construction was installing the exterior wall cover. The exterior beams were made of steel chosen for its strength, not for its visual appeal. These beams were first coated with fireproofing to protect against overheating in the case of an interior fire. At first, asbestos was used, but later it was determined to be a hazardous material. So all the asbestos was removed from the first thirty-five floors, and the project restarted with a safer substance. Then the beams were clad with an aluminum cover, chosen because aluminum reflects light in a luminous, radiant fashion. This would be the face the building would show to the world. In between the beams, tinted, heat-reflective, and extra-heavy-duty glass windows, 43,600 in all, were mounted ten inches in from the exterior wall.

The exterior beams of the Twin Towers featured a reflective aluminum cover, chosen for its luminosity.

Meanwhile, on the lower floors, completion work was under way. The idea was to prepare the building for occupancy up to the first sky lobby even before the entire project was finished. Passenger elevators and escalators were installed. The lobby flooring, wall panels, and light fixtures were handled by a small army of workers. Painting, tiling, and drape hanging were completed on office floors, adding hundreds of workers to the site on any given day.

Just before Christmas in 1970, the north tower "topped out." This is a symbolic step in the erection of any tall building, the moment at which the last piece of the framework steel is put in place. Even though timing is rarely precise enough for the obligatory ceremony to take place at the moment the steel is bolted in, there is always a big party associated with topping out that eventually takes place. Because it was near Christmas, two last columns were hoisted, one adorned (as is traditional) with an American flag, and the other with a Christmas tree.

The first tower was now in place, and seven months later, on July 19, 1971, the second tower topped out. The construction on the south tower had proceeded just like the first tower. The New York skyline now had a new look. But most important, the project overall had been a safe one. Before the World Trade Center was completed, eight workers would die and others would be injured, but that number is generally viewed as fairly low considering that there were as many as thirty-six hundred people on the site on peak days and that the construction took place over several years. Ironworkers do the most dangerous jobs day in and day out because they work with huge and unwieldy pieces of metal, but on the World Trade Center site, not one ironworker was killed. Whether those present at the topping out ceremonies saw the towers as just two more tall buildings or as works of extreme symbolic importance, all on the ground and in the air were full of high spirits. They had done it. It was in the air.

6

LIFE IN THE
CITY IN THE SKY

The official dedication of the World Trade Center in April 1973 was a bit anticlimactic because tenants had begun moving into the building more than two years earlier while it was still under construction. In fact, at the time of the dedication, more than half the office space was already occupied. Life had settled into a routine, although occasionally an inconvenient one because of the chaos and messes caused by the construction. By the mid-1970s, however, the dust had settled and the World Trade Center was functioning smoothly. Likewise, life in the neighborhood, changed forever by the huge plaza and the high towers, had developed a new kind of normalcy.

As the years passed, fewer people who worked and lived in Lower Manhattan remembered life there before the World Trade Center, and much of the controversy surrounding it had subsided. In fact, quite the opposite had occurred: The World Trade Center had become yet another source of pride for many New Yorkers. It was also an important part of the daily lives of tens of thousands of people, whether they worked nearby and strolled to the plaza to eat a lunch they brought from home, took the express elevator to the posh Windows on the World restaurant, or ordered sandwiches to be delivered because they were too busy to leave their offices in the towers.

Yet each individual whose life brought him or her in contact with the World Trade Center saw only the smallest piece of the overall picture. The towers in particular, relatively quiet after business hours and on weekends, were teeming with unseen activity seven days a week, twenty-four hours a day, as a small

People arrive to work at the World Trade Center, which hummed with business activity during weekdays. At night and on weekends, a huge staff kept the complex functioning smoothly.

army of people saw to the smooth functioning of what in many respects was a city in the sky.

A TYPICAL WORKDAY

The routines of the workday were not different for workers in the World Trade Center than they were elsewhere, but they were perhaps in some respects extreme as a result of the fact that fifty thousand people labored side by side in one complex. Those arriving by bus, taxi, or foot would climb a one-story flight of broad stairs to Austin Tobin Plaza, a huge area of concrete and landscaping named for the former executive director of the Port Authority and mastermind of the effort to build the World Trade Center; then they would cross the plaza to the entry to the towers. On many days, movement across the plaza was made more difficult by gusts of wind created by the channeling of moving air into the small area between the towers.

Others arrived at work through the underground concourse, a walkway lined with shops that linked the PATH and other subway lines with the tower lobbies. Many options for grabbing a quick cup of coffee existed there, but because people were in a hurry, they would not wait in lines they perceived would take more than a minute. Behind-the-counter staff bustled to make a sale of coffee and a bite to eat, generally taking no more than twenty seconds. Although the concourse was lined with shops, people in the morning rush hour literally could not stop to window shop because the crowds were so thick they would be pushed along regardless of their wishes. One executive once compared the scene in the corridors of the concourse during the morning rush hour to a "salmon run."[17]

Whether one was an executive or a receptionist, all ran the same gauntlets to get to their offices. By eight or nine o'clock, executives would sit behind huge mahogany desks and clerks would sit in tiny cubicles or open spaces with no privacy, doing the vast range of activities taking place in the towers. Steamship

The impressive lobby entry to the towers is festively decorated for Christmas in 1990.

lines, banks, insurance companies, management companies, engineering firms, law offices, government agencies, and commodities brokers all worked out of the towers.

Lunchtime did not create the kind of rush seen in the morning because many people worked through lunch or ate at their desks, and those who did take a break might do so typically any time between eleven and two or three in the afternoon. For several hours each day, pizza delivery people, juggling as many as a dozen boxes destined for various floors, might have exchanged comments about the weather or the traffic with employees of other fast-food chains carrying orders of sandwiches, Chinese noodles, fried chicken, or hamburgers.

Those who wanted a breath of fresh air might have gone outside to Tobin Plaza to get something to eat from the green and gold fast-food carts, barely noticing the many souvenir stands selling postcards and T-shirts featuring the towers. In the summer, the plaza was particularly lively, with open-air concerts held every workday from around noon to two o'clock. Each day featured a different kind of music, from classical, to Broadway, to country western.

People who needed to use their lunch hour to run errands would have found nearly everything they required at the World Trade Center concourse, below the plaza level. Many national chains were represented, with the majority of shops geared toward purchases women make for themselves and their families. Indeed, 70 percent of those who shopped in the concourse were female, as is true in most malls around the country. But the experience of shopping in the concourse was different. There were no places to sit down and people watch—nothing that could have slowed down the "salmon run" in the morning. People outside the general age of the workforce were rarely seen in the concourse because other places provided a more conducive environment for shopping and strolling, or just hanging out. For example, there was not a single video arcade at the World Trade Center to attract young customers. Another indication that the mall existed primarily for the convenience of the employees at the World Trade Center and the immediate surrounding area was the fact that the hours matched the workday more than they usually do at other shopping centers. Most stores opened at 8:00 A.M. and closed at 6:00 P.M., and remained closed most of the weekend.

The evening rush hour, like lunchtime, was more stretched out than the morning arrival period, which tended to peak between 7:30 and 9:00 A.M. People connected to the stock markets tended to arrive early and leave early, because the stock market

"IT'S HARD TO BE DOWN WHEN YOU'RE UP"

From the earliest stages of planning for the World Trade Center, the Port Authority had struggled to please everyone. As an agency serving the public, it knew it could not afford for the project to sound exclusive. However, it also knew that, to fill the towers with paying tenants, the project would have to be upscale and somewhat elitist. A way of addressing these conflicting priorities became part of the building design: The south tower would be topped by an observation deck open to the public, and the north tower would be topped on its 107th floor by a posh private restaurant club exclusively for tenants and other members during the lunch hour, but open to the public for dinner and on weekends. Controversy broke out over the restaurant's being closed to the public at all, so a compromise was reached that made a few tables available to the public at lunch during the week. This restaurant, Windows on the World, quickly became one of the best known in the United States. Though many considered the food not as good as that of other equally expensive restaurants on the ground, the views were unsurpassed, and it became a popular place to go for special meals and to entertain out-of-town guests.

The observation deck, also on the 107th floor of the other tower, was closed in so it could be used year round. Its opening was kicked off by an advertising campaign featuring the slogan, "It's hard to be down when you're up." When weather conditions permitted, people could take escalators up even higher to an open-air deck set back thirty-one feet from the edge of the roof for safety reasons. Visitors were often struck by the fact that street noise did not reach that height and that for the first time in New York they experienced silence, along with views, on a clear day, stretching more than forty miles. Approximately 2 million people a year visited the observation deck, and it became a popular site for weddings and other important ceremonies.

People enjoy the sunshine during a lunch break in the World Trade Center's plaza.

closes at 4:00 P.M. But many others stayed at work well past the typical 5:00 or 5:30 quitting time. In fact, traffic logs in the towers indicated that occupancy was frequently as high as 30 percent even in the late evening hours, not just because many people's jobs demanded long hours but because those involved with international business must adjust their schedules to the fact that in different time zones around the world the business day is in full swing.

KEEPING THE WORLD TRADE CENTER WORKING

Inside the offices, the workday would pass much as in any other office building. However, behind the scenes, a small army of employees was needed to ensure the smooth functioning of those offices. Every problem with heating or air conditioning, plumbing, and electricity was funneled into one central area in the basement known as the Operations Control Center. There, the phones rang constantly with complaints from burned-out lightbulbs to clogged toilets. Enough people got locked out of offices to keep five locksmiths on the payroll.

DAREDEVILS AT THE TOWERS

"When I see three oranges, I have to juggle. When I see two towers, I have to walk." These words, reported by Judith Dupre in *Skyscrapers*, are the explanation twenty-four-year-old French daredevil Philippe Petit offered for why he made a seventy-five-minute walk on a tightrope between the tops of the Twin Towers on Wednesday, April 7, 1974. The trip of 131 feet took so long because he stopped to lie down, hang by his feet, and jump up and down, to the gasps and admiration of the onlookers below. Petit had been able to set up his feat by posing as a construction worker. This allowed him to leave his supplies at the top of the building, including a crossbow he used to shoot lines from the north to the south tower until a cable strong enough to hold his weight could be strung together. Petit later joined the Barnum and Bailey Circus as a high-wire artist.

A year later, on July 22, 1975, a thirty-four-year-old skydiver, Owen Quinn, parachuted from the top of the north tower to the plaza below. Wind gusts slammed him into the windows, causing cuts and bruises, but he landed safely in less than two minutes—so quickly that only a few people in the building actually saw him streaking by. Later, in an interview, he said his purpose was not for glory but to use the attention he got to make a plea on behalf of the poor.

Two years later, on May 27, 1977, a twenty-seven-year-old amateur mountain climber, George Willig, quickly nicknamed "the human fly," made a three-hour climb to the top of one of the towers. Willig planned the climb for a year, devising special clamps that hooked to the grooves used by the window-washing equipment. While thousands watched and the local media shot videotape, Willig climbed. Eventually, police were lowered from the roof to intercept him, but because he was climbing very competently, they decided, rather than risk grabbing him, they would simply go up alongside him, to rescue him if he faltered. Recognizing the unpopularity of going after a media hero, the city of New York settled on a fine of a penny a floor, or $1.10, which Willig later handed over to Mayor Abe Beame during a noisy news conference.

Tenants submitted approximately forty thousand work orders each year.

Employees maintaining the smooth functioning of the World Trade Center, as contrasted with employees of companies leasing space there, fell into three general categories. The first of these were workers who were rarely if ever seen. In the basement of the towers, huge air conditioning and heating apparatuses had to be monitored and maintained. Backup generators had to be kept in working order for emergencies. Other employees worked on loading docks served by special roads through the basement of the center, where trucks delivered everything from caviar to potato chips, from boxes of paper clips to photocopiers. Still others in basement offices watched closed-circuit television monitors, alerting security to problems requiring their attention.

The second category of building workers was the cleaning crews. To those keeping irregular hours in the buildings, the three or four cleaning people assigned to each floor would have been a familiar sight. Between 4:00 P.M. and midnight, routine office cleaning was done, and from midnight to 8:00 A.M., the common areas such as bathrooms, elevators, the concourse, and the lobbies were cleaned. Work was carried out not by employees of the Port Authority but by privately owned maintenance companies. These employees followed the hundreds of pages of specifications in their contracts. Certain things such as emptying wastebaskets obviously needed to be done every night, but other things that were done far less frequently in smaller buildings, such as a light shampooing of the lobby carpets, also had to be part of the daily routine because of the sheer number of shoes going back and forth across them each day.

The third category of employees was the security staff. Each security officer was assigned certain floors of the building and was expected not only to maintain a constant patrol but also to look for problems requiring the attention of other crews, such as loose tiles, snags in carpets, or odd noises. Other security staff had assigned posts. Those in the lobbies, for example, monitored comings and goings, and issued temporary permits to visitors, a procedure begun after the 1993 bombing of the World Trade Center. Building employees were also required to wear special badges after that event, and problems with those would be handled by lobby security as well. The general operations

WASHING THE WINDOWS

Each side of each tower of the World Trade Center had fifty-eight columns of glass stretching from the ninth floor, above the building entrance, to the 107th floor, where the windows widened to improve the views in the Windows on the World restaurant and the observation deck. To keep the glass clean, a clever window-washing system was designed. Special grooves were fitted into the metal columns of the buildings' exterior, and one window-washing unit per tower used these grooves as tracks, going up and down with a machine that first squirted cleaning solution, then wiped the glass with brushes, and then sucked the cleaning solution back into the machine so that people on the street would not be dripped on. These machines could do twelve columns of windows a day, so it took five days, one workweek, to clean one side. (Between December and mid-March, however, cleaning was not attempted because the water in the units would freeze in the bitter cold.) A special turntable built into the roof of each building moved the machine to the next side the following Monday, and cleaning resumed. At the end of the month, when the whole building had been washed, the process started again.

A window-washing unit scales an exterior wall of one of the towers.

It took an operator on the roof to handle changes from one row and one side of the building to another, but no one had to dangle over the side of the building, a safety feature suggested by architect Minoru Yamasaki, whose fear of heights made him sensitive to this issue.

supervisor made the rounds. He or she was the ranking person on the site and served as the coordinator of all the functions performed by the building staff.

REST AND RELAXATION

While people in the towers and elsewhere around the World Trade Center did their after-hours tasks, from refilling toilet paper, to investigating a theft, to catching up on paperwork after a day of stock market activity, to negotiating a merger with a company in Thailand or Morocco, others were enjoying leisure time in one of the restaurants and bars in the complex. Some were out-of-town businesspeople staying at the Marriott Hotel, which opened as part of the World Trade Center complex in 1981. Others were executives, lawyers, and other New Yorkers stopping with a colleague (or an adversary) for a drink. Others were vacationers who chose to stay in Lower Manhattan.

By late evening, there were two worlds at the World Trade Center. In the subdued post–happy hour crowd in the Marriott Hotel, New Yorkers finished up late dinners and out-of-towners chatted excitedly about the Broadway play they had just seen uptown. In the towers, lights still shone brightly, illuminating the mopping and sweeping, and the mergers and securities trading that would go on all night. Barely visible in the plaza below, if it was a summer night, the homeless tried to catch a little sleep. If wind-driven snow howling between the towers pierced their thin clothing, they headed for the concourse. As long as they kept moving, they were legally entitled to be there. Like everything else about the complex, from the hands pushing the turnstiles of the subway to the hands cleaning the bathroom basins, from the well-groomed hands spending millions with a keystroke to the grimy hands poking through trash cans, movement seemed to symbolize the life of the World Trade Center.

7

IT ALL CAME TUMBLING DOWN

Some were wearing a new outfit they'd bought the night before. Some were having bad hair days or fussing over a few drops of spilled coffee on their clothes. Some were still angry from a fight with their spouse that morning. Some had kissed their newborn babies as they slept, before heading out the door into the predawn darkness. Some had first dates that night. It was someone's birthday, someone's anniversary. Some were wondering what they would make for dinner. Some had left a pile of dirty dishes from last night's dinner at home. Some were young, headed for first jobs on what looked like a promising career path. Some were counting the days till retirement. Some were not coming home.

THE TOWERS FALL

Just before 9:00 A.M. on September 11, 2001, American Airlines Flight 11, en route from Boston to Los Angeles, crashed into the ninety-fourth through the ninety-ninth floors of Tower 1, the north tower of the World Trade Center, where the offices of the financial and insurance firm Marsh and McLennan were located. The seven hundred employees in the main office of securities firm Cantor Fitzgerald, on the 101st through 105th floors, were among those trapped above the wreckage. Among those watching the smoke and flames billowing from the north tower were south tower employees, including employees of the Fuji Bank located on the seventy-ninth through eighty-second floors of Tower 2. Some people used their cell phones to call family or friends to report their bird's-eye view of the breaking news and to reassure their loved ones they were safe. Less than twenty

minutes later, they could only react in horror as a second air-
plane, United Airlines Flight 175, also traveling from Boston to
Los Angeles, buried itself just below them in the seventy-eighth
through eighty-fourth floors. There would be no way for those
above the impact to escape. Whatever happened to the building
would happen to all of them.

*Plumes of smoke billow from the World Trade Center following the cata-
strophic terrorist attacks of September 11, 2001.*

There was no doubt that everyone aboard the two planes and on the floors hit was dead. After all, the planes had simply disappeared inside the buildings. Those below the impact in both towers reacted in a variety of ways. Some stayed where they were, more amazed than frightened; others streamed from the buildings in shock and horror, in some cases having come down by foot seventy or more stories. Firemen rushed into the towers to fight the flames and rescue the trapped occupants, while police officers scrambled to keep order in the streets below. Ambulance sirens were constant.

Few could have imagined that what was about to occur was even possible. The south tower, the second hit, fell first, hesitating a bit at the start, then accelerating to 120 miles per hour as the upper floors hit the ground. Within seconds, it disappeared into a storm of its own debris, which barreled down the nearby streets. Cars, ambulances, and people near the site were buried; those fleeing the scene were covered with a choking cloud of dust. Less than a half hour later, the north tower followed its twin. By 10:30, it was all over. The two tallest buildings in New York, the fifth and sixth largest in the world, lay in rubble. Approximately three thousand people who had fallen with them were entombed inside. An entire nation watched in stunned silence, trying to comprehend the finality of it all.

SURVIVING THE BLOW

For a little over an hour after the second crash, the south tower had stood. The north tower stood longer, for more than an hour and a half. It may have seemed to many, when the towers appeared to have absorbed the impact, that once the fires were put out, the problem would be how to extricate the remains of two planes from the buildings, recover the bodies, repair the damage, and go on with business. Today, some architects point out that the fact that one tower stood for an hour and the other over an hour and a half without collapsing is evidence not of weakness but of the extraordinary strength of Yamasaki's design. Approximately 25,000 people had time to get out of the buildings safely before they collapsed. However, the structure was also undergoing stresses unimagined by its architect. The physical processes were so powerful that the fate of the buildings and the people in them was already sealed even while the buildings seemed briefly to stand firm.

When a building is destroyed as utterly as the Twin Towers were, architects and engineers lose much of the evidence that would be helpful in diagnosing the structural failure. Within a month, however, they were beginning to propose theories based on a meticulous analysis of videotapes of the collapses, computer simulations, and clues found in the debris. They knew that

"I SAW THINGS NO ONE SHOULD EVER SEE"

"I know 40 people who work on the 106th floor. They're just not there anymore. I saw 5 people jump from the window. It was just horrible." The speaker's daughter grips his hand and says, "But Mommy works in the World Trade Center." He answers, "Well, we hope Mommy is all right." This story is among those told in the MSNBC article "I Saw Things No One Should Ever See," published two days after the attack. A fireman reported seeing a body fall through the ceiling and land at his feet as he entered one of the towers. Firefighters climbed over piles of debris. "There's a part of a body over there," one said. "Was it in uniform?" another asked. A student who lived nearby saw at least seven people jump. "You can see a person going straight down, no floating or anything. It's the sickest thing you've ever seen in your whole life." Trauma surgeons, who by coincidence were holding a conference at nearby Madison Square Garden, rushed to the area to help. They soon realized there would be no one who needed them. "We haven't seen any wounded," one said. "You're either going to walk out of there or you're dead."

A young architect recalled that "You couldn't move. It was like being in a dark room." The streets and trees were littered with metal, paper, and other materials. "I could feel the debris up to my knees," she said. Another nearby resident watching from his window said, "All I could see was all the fire and smoke and bits of paper and building floating around like confetti. I saw 15 or 20 people literally jump . . . to their deaths." "There were body parts for blocks," said a fireman. "Every time you looked up someone was jumping. I guess when you're burning alive you do stupid things." Several firefighters leaned against a trashed car, saying, "There's people still alive in there. There's got to be. This is helplessness."

the tightly spaced outer columns had been stiff enough to bear the weight above them indefinitely. The stiffness of these outer columns was also what kept the buildings from tipping over from a sideways, or lateral, impact the equivalent of 25 million pounds. Each of the planes, 156 feet wide from wing tip to wing tip, tore out about three dozen exterior columns, but the surviving columns formed an arch, called a Vierendeel truss, over the damage, distributing weight around the missing columns well enough to prevent quick collapse.

According to MIT engineer Tomasz Wierzbiecki, a specialist in impact and crashworthiness of structures, the wings and fuselage, or body, of the aircraft were made of thin enough metal that the impact of the crash would have "shredded [them] into pieces the size of an adult's fist."[18] However, the more solid parts of the plane such as the engines would have continued forward at high speed and hit the inner core columns, weakening or breaking probably slightly less than half of them. Even though the building supports were undoubtedly severely damaged both at the center and at the exterior, there would have been at least a long enough window of time to rescue everyone inside, and possibly enough time to come in and make emergency repairs.

WHY THE TOWERS FELL

In short, most believe the towers could have survived the impact of the planes. The problem lay in the ten thousand gallons of jet fuel that had ignited in the crash. Jet fuel burns at very high heat—much higher than the heat generated by fires fueled only by typical flammable materials found in buildings such as curtains, furniture, wood paneling, and the like. Minoru Yamasaki had designed the Twin Towers using only a steel framework to support their weight. His innovative use of core and exterior weight-bearing columns without inner pillars was applauded at the time, but it did contribute in the end to the buildings' collapse. Steel softens with heat, and it conducts that heat far beyond the original source. Yamasaki's buildings had nothing but steel bearing their weight. If the steel gave way, the building would have nothing holding it up. Since Yamasaki's time, architects have recognized this problem and have turned to weight-bearing systems that combine steel with concrete or some other material, but when the World Trade Center was constructed, these materials were associated with the heavier looking skyscrapers of the past and were bypassed in favor of the light and airy look of glass and metal.

Most architects and engineers agree that the first step in the collapse was the weakening of the steel trusses that held up the poured concrete floors on the stories where the heat from

AMONG THE DEAD

Approximately three thousand people perished in the attack on the World Trade Center. Though this number is far smaller than it would have been if so many people had not used the time the towers remained standing to escape to safety, it is still the highest number of people lost in one day in U.S. history, more than even the worst day of the deadliest battle of the Civil War. Among the dead were ninety-six individuals whose last names started with the letter "A" alone. The youngest among this group were Thomas Ashton, a twenty-one-year-old electrician, starting only his second day of training, who was working at the north tower alongside an experienced electrician on one of the floors directly hit; Terence Adderly, a twenty-two-year-old staff member at Fred Alger Management Company on the ninety-third floor, one story below the direct impact at the north tower; Laura Angilletta, a twenty-three-year-old clerk at Cantor Fitzgerald; and Telmo Alvear, a twenty-five-year-old waiter at Windows on the World. Alvear left behind a one-year-old child. He had finished the night shift and was only in the building because he had agreed to cover a friend's shift. Both Angilletta and Alvear waited out the last minutes of their lives trapped above the impact at the north tower.

Among the oldest were firefighter Joseph Angelini, sixty-three, whose son by the same name was also killed; Angelo Amaranto, a sixty-year-old custodian who had worked at the World Trade Center for thirty-one years; Ignatius Adanga, sixty-two, of the New York State Department of Transportation; and seventy-four-year-old Jeremiah Ahern of the New York State Department of Taxation and Finance, who was trapped above the wreckage in the south tower.

A massive pile of rubble remains after the terrorist attacks. Analysts have not yet agreed on why the towers collapsed completely, when only a few floors near the top were impacted by the suicide planes.

the fire was most intense. Steel begins to soften at 1,100 degrees Fahrenheit, and the fires in the towers reached higher than 2,000 degrees within a few seconds. As the steel heated up, it softened and, just like spaghetti in a pot, began to sag. The softened steel was forced downward by the weight of the concrete floor it supported, causing stress on the connections between the trusses and the core and exterior columns. These connections, formed by pairs of three-quarter-inch bolts and strong welds, stressed by heat themselves and by the downward pressure of the weight of the floor, eventually tore free from the columns, sending the floor downward.

Those studying the disaster generally agree with this analysis of the initial stage of the collapse. However, there is no clear consensus on what caused a local collapse on a few floors to bring the whole building to the ground. There may never be such a consensus, but one leading theory proposes that each floor added weight to what the trusses on the floor

RUDOLPH GIULIANI

For most New Yorkers, memories of the catastrophe that befell the city on September 11, 2001, will include Rudolph Giuliani. A former prosecutor, Giuliani became mayor in 1993. His time in office was considered quite successful because his focus on reducing crime had turned New York into one of the safer large cities in the United States. Though Giuliani was well respected, he had been beset in the months before the disaster by a bout with prostate cancer as well as a tabloid scandal involving an extramarital relationship and its role in the breakup of his marriage. He was also near the end of his term-limited time as mayor. Most people felt that Giuliani had already accomplished all that he was going to, and they were focusing on the upcoming election that would determine who would replace him. Then disaster struck. Within hours, Giuliani was holding news conferences aimed at calming the people and assuring them that the city was still functioning.

Ernest Hemingway once defined courage as "grace under pressure," and Giuliani illustrated that kind of courage. He visited the site of the former World Trade Center regularly in the ensuing days and kept his word to keep people informed. Giuliani was everyone's mayor, which he demonstrated by attending dozens of funerals—and not just those of the most prominent victims—prayer vigils, and mass memorial services.

New York mayor Rudolph Giuliani was a tower of hope and strength for his city and for the nation.

Giuliani ran into trouble with the firefighters and other officers a month or so after the disaster when he decided to cut back on the number of people involved in the recovery effort. This was seen as disrespectful to those who had died in the line of duty and insensitive to the number of hours of their own time firemen and other uniformed officers had already put in for that purpose. They felt they were owed more support, and several were arrested in a scuffle over the issue at the site. Though he was not able to regain their confidence, most of the rest of New York will remember the days and weeks after the disaster as Giuliani's finest hours. In fact, at the end of 2001, Giuliani was honored by being selected *Time*'s Person of the Year.

below, themselves weakened by conducted heat, had to support and that the floors simply separated and fell, somewhat
like pulling down a zipper. The force yanking the bolts free
destabilized the columns, toppling them inward and adding
their rubble to the weight going down.

Contributing to the collapse of the columns was their inher-
ent instability. A basic principle of architecture worked out with
the first skyscrapers, medieval cathedrals, is that tall walls need
to be laterally braced or they will topple. In modern high rises,
the support for a building also works both horizontally and ver-
tically. The columns hold up the floors, but the floors also serve
as lateral support for the columns. Therefore, when the floors of
the Twin Towers fell, there was no way that the columns could
stand independently. The exterior ones probably fell more easily, but apparently the momentum of the fall was enough to pull
down the heavily damaged core columns as well. When they
fell, the undamaged parts of the buildings had nothing holding
them up in the middle and they fell too. At a certain point, the
weight of the building combined with the speed of the fall

Firemen and police face the challenge of dealing with the collapse of the towers.

AMERICA'S NEWEST HEROES

Most firefighters shrug off being called heroes for their efforts to save lives and property, saying that, after all, it's just their job. When it was revealed that the casualties of the disaster included several hundred members of the Fire Department of New York, people knew that these deaths were somehow different from the rest, and the firefighters, along with other uniformed officers from the police, paramedics, and Port Authority, were quickly idealized as heroes. Firefighters in full gear rushed from the safety of the streets into the towers while hundreds of other people were streaming out; they chose to be there to attempt rescues and save the building if possible despite the obvious danger. Whole companies and squads were lost when the towers collapsed around them.

In all, 343 firemen died at the World Trade Center, approximately 7 percent of the total deaths. This figure is brought into perspective by the fact that a total of 774 firefighters had died in the line of duty between 1865 and September 11, so on this one day the number who perished was almost half that total. Among the dead were several high-ranking officers, including Fire Chief Peter Ganci, fifty-four, the highest-ranking uniformed officer in the department and a thirty-five-year veteran of the department; he died in a thunder of debris while supervising evacuations. First Department Fire Commissioner William Feehan, seventy-one, a forty-year veteran of the force and the second-highest-ranking person in the fire department, was also killed at his command post when one of the towers collapsed on him. Another death to which special attention was paid was that of Fire Department Chaplain Mychal Judge, sixty-eight, who was struck in the head and killed by falling debris while administering last rites to a victim.

became sufficient, even without the element of heat, to "pancake" the remaining floors.

GROUND ZERO

On the afternoon of September 11, 2001, all that remained of the Twin Towers was a seven-story-high burning pile of rubble containing, in addition to the structural steel, 200,000 lighting fixtures, 400 miles of conduit, and 7 million square feet of flooring. The greatest horror, of course, was that the debris also covered thousands of people, some of them possibly still alive but out of reach. Building 7, constructed in 1987, and

Building 5, both containing additional insurance, financial, and other businesses, were destroyed, too, as was Building 3, the New York Marriott World Trade Center Hotel. Building 4, the Commodities Exchange, and Building 6, the United States Custom House, had both partially collapsed. The site was

Police, firefighters, and other workers pause for prayers at Ground Zero.

quickly nicknamed "Ground Zero" for its similarity to the spot on which a nuclear bomb is detonated. Other New Yorkers preferred a boxing analogy and began calling the event and the scene simply "the punch." Whatever one called it, it was a nightmarish scene. The greasy dust clouds carried traces of human ashes and the remains of the papers they had filed, the desks at which they had sat, and the carpets on which they had walked. The air was seared with the smell of melting, burning, and rotting.

The extent of the damage above ground was obvious, but additional concerns were quickly voiced about what might have occurred underground. Debris filled the basement floors, and there was initially some concern that the "bath-tub" constructed to keep the construction site and the below-ground levels of the building dry might have been damaged. This would have created many more problems, because a breech in its concrete wall would have resulted in more than sixty feet of water pooling below and inside the lower floors of the building, including the PATH terminal. Water in the terminal could have flooded far more extensive sections of the subway system, extending damage and disruption well beyond the World Trade Center site. The excavation proceeded more cautiously than it might otherwise have had to in order to be sure that, like in a game of Pick Up Sticks, moving one thing did not inadvertently move something else that was propping up yet something else, unleashing potentially disastrous results.

COMING TO GRIPS WITH LOSS

Volunteers and paid workers alike lent untold hours of time to what was first a rescue mission but, within a few weeks, had become an effort to clear the site and find whatever fragments of the dead still existed. Many of the same people, or their children, worked to carry away what they once had helped build. "I worked . . . from '70 to '71," said one steelworker at the scene. "I told my kids I built the tallest buildings in the world."[19] Another ironworker not yet born when the towers were built echoed the admiration ironworkers feel for their union brothers who put together the towers: "For us, the higher [a building] gets, the more bragging rights. You worked the Twin Towers, you're the man." His grandfather, who had fitted steel on the tops of the buildings, told him, "They took it down, now you get a chance to put it back up."[20]

But first the dust had to settle, not just at the site but, figuratively speaking, across the nation, as Americans grasped for words to express their thoughts and many acknowledged they were not yet quite sure what those thoughts were. Beyond grief, fury, fright, and despair, Americans were numb as they struggled to come to grips with exactly what they had lost and what it meant to their future.

EPILOGUE

If a person stood right at the corner of one of the Twin Towers and looked straight up along its edge, the height would trick the eye into seeing just a thin, gray line. "One of the most massive buildings of the modern era" would, in the words of Eric Darton, "perform its built-in vanishing act."[21] Now there is no place to stand at the foot of the building to try this experiment, or perhaps more accurately, one can now stand anywhere, for the disappearance is real, and it is total.

The enormity of this fact has left New Yorkers and others struggling to find analogies as a way of comprehending the incomprehensible. "It's like watching . . . two close friends assassinated before your eyes," says artist Julien LaVerdiere. He adds that the towers are "still the phantom limbs of the city."[22] Admittedly, the towers were not almost universally loved in the same way a few other symbols of New York, such as the Empire State Building or the Statue of Liberty. They were simply there, inseparable from people's vision of the city, two perfect rectangles winning the contest to reach the sky. It is their loss that has clarified their importance.

Losses cry out to be filled, but the question of what to put on the World Trade Center site is a complex one. Some argue that the towers should be rebuilt just as they were, as a way of saying that America remains intact, like a fighter who staggers back to his feet to show that the blow that knocked him down didn't hurt him. Others are quick to point out that the project was highly controversial at the outset and not an unqualified success in the end, and to rebuild it is to lose the chance to do something better. Some propose that the site be preserved as a memorial park. One suggestion, made by LaVerdiere and his partner Paul Myoda, is to create huge columns of light beaming upward where the buildings once stood, "a luminescent column . . . soothing the nation's wound, [covering] that giant scar in the sky."[23] Hundreds of ideas have so far been proposed, having in common only a sincere wish that the dead be respected and that the strength of the country be pronounced loudly and clearly.

Practically speaking, however, the land on which the World Trade Center stood is too valuable not to return to commercial use. Though undoubtedly whatever is built will incorporate a memorial, there will almost certainly be companies doing business on the site within a few years. In 1998, the Port Authority, which still owns the land, turned over the operation of the World Trade Center to a private leaseholder who has already announced his desire to build a new office complex on the site. Architect David Childs's firm has been hired to design whatever goes up in the World Trade Center's place. "This city has rebuilt itself continuously," Childs argues. "Buildings come down and new ones go up. We preserve the best of our past, and then we constantly shift as our culture changes."[24]

Buildings do indeed come down in New York, but not in the way these did. When a building is carefully imploded to make way for a new one, no psyches are hurt to the core, no lifestyle challenged, no values are reexamined. No one is supposed to die. American culture does change, and as Childs correctly points out, its buildings reflect this. Life in the United States clearly changed when the towers fell, but most feel it is too soon to say exactly how.

More than two months after the Twin Towers fell, their ruins

The Manhattan skyline after the terrorist attacks. The absence of the Twin Towers is a grim reminder of the terrible events of September 11.

still smoldered. The rubble was so deep that officials predicted it would take a year to clear. Perhaps it is apt that it would take that much time for the pieces of steel and glass to be picked up, and the remains of the people who fell with the building to be identified and honored. A year is the traditional period of mourning in many of the cultures from which the United States has been shaped. In the aftermath of September 11, 2001, a whole nation was bereaved. Just as the backhoes and cranes pick up the pieces, so must those who lost loved ones, and so do the millions of others whose loss was more abstract.

Something else will take the World Trade Center's place in time. Undoubtedly, it will be controversial, just as its predecessor was. In its own way, though, it will redefine New York and the country, just as the towers did when they first rose in a time when even the sky did not seem like the limit to the dreams of a nation.

NOTES

Introduction
1. Dan Rather, *CBS News*, September 11, 2001.

Chapter 1: The Shaping of a City
2. Eric Darton, *Divided We Stand: A Biography of New York's World Trade Center*. New York: Basic Books, 1999, p. 9.
3. Darton, *Divided We Stand*, p. 9.
4. Darton, *Divided We Stand*, p. 12.
5. Quoted in Darton, *Divided We Stand*, p. 12.

Chapter 2: The Deal Is Sealed: Port Politics
6. Quoted in Darton, *Divided We Stand*, p. 46.
7. Quoted in Angus Kress Gillespie, *Twin Towers: The Life of New York City's World Trade Center*. New Brunswick, NJ: Rutgers University Press, 1999, p. 46.
8. Darton, *Divided We Stand*, p. 110.

Chapter 3: Going Down: Preparing to Build
9. Gillespie, *Twin Towers*, p. 61.
10. Gillespie, *Twin Towers*, p. 71.
11. Gillespie, *Twin Towers*, p. 74.

Chapter 4: Solving the Problems of Size
12. Gillespie, *Twin Towers*, p. 78.

Chapter 5: Going Up: Construction and Complications
13. Quoted in Gillespie, *Twin Towers*, p. 119.
14. Gillespie, *Twin Towers*, p. 89.
15. Gillespie, *Twin Towers*, p. 93.
16. Quoted in Gillespie, *Twin Towers*, p. 93.

Chapter 6: Life in the City in the Sky
17. Quoted in Gillespie, *Twin Towers*, p. 212.

Chapter 7: It All Came Tumbling Down
18. Quoted in James Glanz, "Why Trade Center Towers Stood, Then Fell," *New York Times On The Web*, November 11, 2001. www.nytimes.com.
19. Quoted in "The Sad Tale of the Iron Workers," MSNBC, September 14, 2001. www.msnbc.com.

20. Quoted in "The Sad Tale of the Iron Workers."

Epilogue

21. Darton, *Divided We Stand*, p. 4.

22. Quoted in "Rebuilding the Twin Towers," MSNBC, October 21, 2001. www.msnbc.com.

23. Quoted in "Rebuilding the Twin Towers."

24. Quoted in "Rebuilding the Twin Towers."

GLOSSARY

aesthetics: The study of the nature of beauty, art, and taste, and people's appreciation and enjoyment of them.

curtain wall: An architectural term used to describe an exterior wall that does not bear weight but serves only as the necessary barrier between the outside and inside of a building.

girder cage: A boxlike structure of horizontal girders connected to and supporting vertical pillars or columns designed to distribute weight evenly in a large, heavy structure.

grillage: A gridlike cage of metal rods used to reinforce panels of concrete.

masonry: Construction using brick or stone.

setbacks: An architectural term used to describe construction in which upper floors are less massive in size than those on lower levels, forming smaller tiers as the building rises.

slurry trench: An excavation method used in wet areas in which a slurry, or thin, mudlike mixture, replaces excavated material to keep walls from flooding or collapsing.

For Further Reading

Books

Shirley Climo, *City! New York*. New York: Macmillan, 1990. This volume from the series about American cities is lively and descriptive, focusing primarily on Manhattan.

Jim Davis and Sharryl Davis Hawke, *New York*. Austin, TX: Raintree-Steck-Vaughan, 1990. Strong on background information about the city and famous residents, past and present.

Eric Hornsberger, *Historical Atlas of New York City*. New York: Henry Holt, 1998. Double-page spreads combine maps, illustrations, and text to develop the history of the city around themes and specific subjects.

Kenneth T. Jackson, *The Encyclopedia of New York City*. New Haven, CT: Yale University Press, 1995. The most complete reference volume on New York City available today, containing four thousand entries and almost seven hundred maps and illustrations.

David MacAulay, *Unbuilding*. New York: Houghton Mifflin, 1986. Through this whimsical but educational story about a man who wants to move the Empire State Building and has to take it apart piece by piece, the reader learns a great deal about the architecture of skyscrapers.

Duncan Michael and Ray Carpenter, *How Skyscrapers Are Made*. New York: Facts On File, 1987. Informative book about the architectural and engineering aspects of building skyscrapers.

Chris Oxlade, *Skyscrapers and Towers*. Austin, TX: Raintree-Steck-Vaughan, 1996. Another well-written book about the construction of high-rise buildings.

Websites:

CNN (CNN.com). Good basic site for current news and archived articles on the World Trade Center.

Legacy.com (www.legacy.com). A site devoted to the people who died on September 11, 2001, including biographical sketches, newspaper obituaries, and photos, as well as notes and re-membrances by those who knew them.

MSNBC (msnbc.com). Another good site for ongoing information.

New York Times On The Web (www.nytimes.com). A particularly good newspaper source because of its New York location.

New York's World Trade Center: A Living Archive (www.ericdarton.net). Extremely good resource for information, including a site for postings and discussion.

VIDEOTAPE:

World Trade Center. Don Cambou, director; Bruce Nash, pro-ducer. *History Channel*, October 2001. Excellent documen-tary about the history of the World Trade Center, filmed before its destruction, with a new introduction and com-mentary by Harry Smith.

WORKS CONSULTED

BOOKS

Mario Campi, *Skyscrapers: An Architectural Type of Modern Urbanism*. Basel, Germany: Birkhauser Press, 2000. Contains a good but brief discussion of the construction and functions of the World Trade Center.

Eric Darton, *Divided We Stand: A Biography of New York's World Trade Center*. New York: Basic Books, 1999. Excellent and thorough discussion of the political and other controversies surrounding the development of the World Trade Center, with good historical and sociological background about the city.

Judith Dupre, *Skyscrapers*. New York: Black Dog and Leventhal, 1996. Though there are only a few pages on the World Trade Center, the material contains anecdotes and background not often included in brief discussions.

Angus Kress Gillespie, *Twin Towers: The Life of New York City's World Trade Center*. New Brunswick, NJ: Rutgers University Press, 1999. Thorough discussion of the building of the World Trade Center, including numerous profiles of the individuals involved.

Eric P. Nash, *Manhattan Skyscrapers*. New York: Princeton Architectural Press, 1999. Short discussion of the World Trade Center, but a valuable means of putting the project in historical and architectural context.

Mario Salvadori, *Why Buildings Stand Up: The Strength of Architecture*. New York: W. W. Norton, 1980. Very readable book about building principles, including a chapter on the architecture of skyscrapers.

Ivan Zaknis and Matthew Smith, *100 of the World's Tallest Buildings*. Corte Madera, CA: Gingko Press, 1998. Another short discussion containing a good description of the World Trade Center's architectural and decorative style.

WEBSITES:

Firehouse.com. www.firehouse.com. One of several websites maintained by firefighters around the country; includes slide shows and other information about the events at the World Trade Center.

James Glanz, "Why Trade Center Towers Stood, Then Fell," *New York Times On The Web*, November 11, 2001. www. nytimes.com.

"I Saw Things No One Should Ever See," MSNBC, September 13, 2001. www.msnbc.com.

"Rebuilding the Twin Towers," MSNBC, October 21, 2001. www.msnbc.com.

"The Sad Tale of the Iron Workers," MSNBC, September 14, 2001. www.msnbc.com.

INDEX

Picture Credits

Cover photos: (left) Associated Press/AP; (upper right)
  © Catherine Karnow/CORBIS); (lower right) © AFP/CORBIS
© AFP/CORBIS, 34, 89
Associated Press, AP, 49, 84
© Bettmann/CORBIS, 18, 28, 31, 32, 71
Brown Brothers, 23
Getty Images News Services, 39
© John Heseltine/CORBIS, 81
Hulton/Archive by Getty Images, 14, 16, 20, 62, 69
Chris Jouan, 42, 47, 53, 56
© Craig Lovell/CORBIS, 74
PhotoDisc, 11
© Reuters NewMedia Inc./CORBIS, 90, 91, 93
© Charles E. Rotkin/CORBIS, 27, 60
© Shepard Sherbell/CORBIS, 97
© G.E. Kidder Smith/CORBIS, 51
© Adam Woolfitt/CORBIS, 65
© Michael S. Yamashita/CORBIS, 75, 78

About the Author

Laurel Corona lives in Lake Arrowhead, California, and teaches English and humanities at San Diego City College. She has a master's degree from the University of Chicago and a Ph.D. from the University of California at Davis. Dr. Corona has written many other books for Lucent Books, including *Brazil*, *Ethiopia*, *Life in Moscow*, *Norway*, and *Peru*.